99

B2 | *K*

Y

"Bright, breezy, and wearing his learning lightly, historian Catherwood has crafted a most illuminating cross-sectional review of the global evangelical movement as it is today. I found it unputdownable; I think many others will too."

J. I. Packer, Professor of Theology, Regent College; author, *Knowing God*

"Christopher Catherwood knows history, but not the dry and dusty kind. This book tells a living story in a lively way. It is a kind of 'editorial meets story time.' Christopher has all that you need to write a compelling book—style and information, specific examples and opinions. And he knows everyone! So this is not a dry 'book for the ages'; this is a book for today. If you want to know who evangelicals are and what they're about, this book will tell you—and this man knows what he's talking about."

Mark Dever, Senior Pastor, Capitol Hill Baptist Church, Washington, DC

"*The Evangelicals* is a good book to give those who know of this purportedly weird tribe only from sensationalistic new stories. Christopher Catherwood's easy-to-read style makes this introduction to evangelical thought and practice like a cup of chamomile tea at bedtime–and it won't produce any nightmares."

Marvin Olasky, Editor-in-chief, *World*; Provost, King's College, New York City

"An eye-opening, stereotype-destroying account of worldwide evangelicalism. Catherwood demonstrates the breadth and dynamism of evangelicals and paints a quite different—and more accurate—picture of them than that often still embraced by secular academics and the secular media—and at times by evangelicals themselves."

Steve Monsma, Research Fellow, the Henry Institute
for the Study of Christianity and Politics, Calvin College;
author, *Healing for a Broken World: Christian Perspectives on Public Policy*

"Christopher Catherwood's insider credentials and global contacts make his a voice worth heeding in the evangelical movement. He offers a hopeful take on a God-graced phenomenon spreading worldwide. His critical take on distinctive American traits in evangelicalism will prompt serious reflection."

Collin Hansen, author of
Young, Restless, Reformed: A Journalist's Journey with the New Calvinists

The Evangelicals

WHAT THEY BELIEVE,

WHERE THEY ARE,

AND THEIR POLITICS

CHRISTOPHER CATHERWOOD

:: CROSSWAY

WHEATON, ILLINOIS

The Evangelicals: What They Believe, Where They Are, and Their Politics
Copyright © 2010 by Christopher Catherwood
Published by Crossway
        1300 Crescent Street
        Wheaton, Illinois 60187

Published in association with the literary agency of RoperPenberthy Publishing Ltd., 19 Egerton Place, Weybidge, Surrey, KT13 0PF, England.

Interior design and typesetting: Lakeside Design Plus
Cover design and illustration: Tobias' Outerwear for Books
First printing 2010
Printed in the United States of America

Trade Paperback ISBN:	978-1-4335-0401-3
PDF ISBN:	978-1-4335-1247-6
Mobipocket ISBN:	978-1-4335-1248-3
ePub ISBN:	978-1-4335-2281-9

Library of Congress Cataloging-in-Publication Data
    Catherwood, Christopher.
        The evangelicals : what they believe, where they are, and their politics / Christopher Catherwood.
        p. cm.
    Includes bibliographical references (p.   ).
    ISBN 978-1-4335-0401-3 (tp)
    1. Evangelicalism. I. Title.

BR1640.C38 2010
270.8'2—dc22

                   2010001690

Crossway is a publishing ministry of Good News Publishers.

VP		21	20	19	18	17	16	15	14	13	12		11	10
14	13	12	11	10	9	8	7	6	5	4	3		2	1

With fondest memories
of St. Ebbe's 73-76

To Keith Weston,
former rector of St. Ebbe's, Oxford,
and his wife Margaret

To Mark Ashton,
vicar of St. Andrew the Great, Cambridge,
and his wife Fiona

To Giles Walter,
vicar of St. John's, Tunbridge Wells,
and his wife Sarah

And to my very favorite evangelical,
my wife,
Paulette

Contents

Preface

A trendy new theory says that where you were raised influences the rest of your life. For example, Bill Gates lived near one of the few schools at the time that had a computer, and tennis stars Venus and Serena Williams were raised near one of the rare tennis courts in their part of Los Angeles.

I am not sure about whether this theory always works, but it can be applied to my own life. I was raised in an evangelical church in London that was one of the few at the time that had a very international congregation. People from every inhabited continent would come faithfully every Sunday, and this was back in the 1950s. (Today another high profile evangelical church in London, All Souls Church, Langham Place, has a congregation that is 45 percent from outside the United Kingdom, many members being from Africa, Asia, and Latin America).

Then from the ages of around eighteen to twenty-six I was involved in the International Fellowship of Evangelical Students (IFES). This really does have members from every inhabited part of the planet, and I would go each year as a British delegate to its international student conference, in Austria, where fellow students from dozens of different countries and continents would convene annually for two to three weeks at a time.

Now my wife and I attend a similarly internationally oriented church in Cambridge, itself a very cosmopolitan kind of place; the college that

I use for my social base, St. Edmund's, regularly has students from over sixty countries in any given academic year.

So in a real sense I have been raised with the tale I am telling in this book: that evangelicalism is truly a multinational, multicultural, interdenominational body of every race, social class, and political persuasion that one can imagine, and not the white, Anglo-Saxon, English-speaking, and politically far-to-the-right-of-center body that the press often describes it as being. Many Brazilian evangelicals have views that would put them almost on the Marxist end of the political spectrum, yet they can have fellowship with a white American who has voted Republican all of his or her life.

I have therefore been fascinated by the issues raised in this book since childhood, and have been actively involved in the wider evangelical world for over thirty-six years. In recent times authors such as Philip Jenkins have described the global evangelical renaissance in academic terms and have brought it to the attention of the university world, at least, if not to the media, where the old clichés still, alas, persist. But for me the astonishing growth of evangelicalism over the past few decades has paralleled my own life experience, as I visited fellow evangelicals in Central America, the Middle East, behind the Iron Curtain pre-1989, and in China and other parts of East Asia. What books now tell you are things I have seen with my own eyes.

Therefore when Richard Roper and Allan Fisher asked me to write this book, I was delighted to accept their offer in the hope that my readers would get a picture of what the evangelical world is *really* like as opposed to the rather distorted media view that is certainly based upon ignorance and probably upon strong bias as well.

I hope that my readers will end up as excited by one of the biggest global phenomena of the twenty-first century as I am. Enjoy the book!

Acknowledgments

For some strange reason, the most important person in the acknowledgments—the author's spouse—is often left until the very end. This is a shame, and one that some of us in Cambridge have been careful to try to change in the books we write.

So I am therefore most happy to begin mine with my wife Paulette. She is my constant companion, best friend, muse, support, inspiration, lady from Proverbs (she descends, apart from anything else, from Virginian pioneer stock), and source of endless wisdom, love, and helpfulness. And that is only the beginning.

The idea for this book came from one of the most-liked people in the British Christian book trade, Richard Roper, someone who has been a firm friend now for well over a quarter of a century (yes, we *are* getting that old) and is still as instrumental in getting books into print as when I first met him as a novice in his first job all those years ago. My thanks to him, to his wife Grace, and to their family are long-lasting.

I am also blessed with my US publisher: editor Allan Fisher, whose joining Crossway some years back was splendid news to many of us authors, let alone to his new employer, and to that wonderful couple without whom Crossway would not be as it is today, Lane and Ebeth Dennis, who have so thankfully kept the faith when many have begun to slide. I will soon celebrate my silver anniversary as a Crossway author, and I am as grateful to them as ever.

The dedication is to some of those pastors, past and present, under whom I have had the privilege of sitting on many a Sunday since my first day as an undergraduate back in the 1970s. Keith and Margaret Weston at St. Ebbe's in Oxford and Mark and Fiona Ashton at St. Andrew the Great in Cambridge, are, with Mark's former curate, Giles Walter and his wife Sarah, models of what proper pastor and wife teams ought to be, whether based on biblical criteria or those of the more recent decrees of the Church of England (to whose original evangelical faith and doctrine all six have kept loyal). My thanks to all of them is profound.

When I signed the contract for this book, Mark Ashton was in glowing health. But when I was halfway through writing it, he was diagnosed with a particularly severe and usually inoperable form of cancer. By the time you read this he may no longer be alive. He has been my longest pastor—longer even than the great Dr. D. Martyn Lloyd-Jones of Westminster Chapel in London (my late maternal grandfather), who retired from that pulpit when I was thirteen. Mark has been my pastor for eighteen years, every day of which I have been grateful to God for the ministry that he has so faithfully carried out in Cambridge.

I also thank Dr. Mark Dever of Capitol Hill Baptist Church in Washington, DC, whose church I have used and whose splendid 9 Marks of a Healthy Church program I have also used to show what a real evangelical church is, or certainly should be, like. Mark, along with his wife Connie, changed my life. Many years ago the two of them introduced me to an American friend of theirs called Paulette, and she is now my wife! So my thanks to Mark cannot be profound enough! Now he embodies what evangelical ministry should be all about in the United States in the same way that Mark Ashton has done for so long in Britain.

I could not be more blessed in my evangelical heritage. I am deeply thankful to my parents, Fred and Elizabeth Catherwood, who are not only models of all that concerned and godly Christian parents should be, but who through their work with the International Fellowship of Evangelical Students for over sixty years have modeled what evangelical faith should be to thousands throughout those decades. Likewise I am grateful for my grandparents, Martyn and Bethan Lloyd-Jones, both no longer with us, but who in their own time showed the world what evangelicals should be.

I am most grateful to the weekly prayerful support of my home group at St. Andrew the Great. In addition to my wife, the members have been: Richard and Sally Reynolds, two wonderfully encouraging friends to whom my first bestseller (on Winston Churchill) is rightly dedicated; Derek Wright; our hosts Matthew and Sarah Burling, Jane Hollis, and Juliet Cook; and former home group members Falcon Green and Max and Julia Halbert. The staff of the International Fellowship of Evangelical Students has been magnificent. I am especially indebted to Las Newman, the former acting general secretary and long-term staff member, and to Kirsty Thorburn, the administrator without whose unstinting hard work over many years things would never have happened. Warmest thanks to so great a team!

I am also thankful to those people on both sides of the Atlantic who receive my prayer e-mails—thank you for your prayerful long-distance support. My wife's many friends in Virginia and my old friends from university days have been a splendid source of Christian fellowship and encouragement these past thirty-five years and more.

Cambridge University Library is an excellent repository of books, and I have profited from its copyright library status. I am grateful to the many places in Cambridge where I work and teach: St. Edmund's College Cambridge, a place with many distinguished evangelicals on their fellowship who prove that international scientific eminence and evangelical faith are fully compatible (special thanks to the former master, Sir Brian Heap, an erstwhile foreign secretary and vice president of the Royal Society and former president of the Institute of Biology, as well as an outstanding evangelical thinker and ethicist); Homerton College Cambridge (where many of my students have been of firm evangelical faith); Churchill College Cambridge (where a strongly evangelical member of the archives staff was at the desk as I was writing this); and to the INSTEP program of several US universities on this side of the Big Pond, for whom I have the pleasure of teaching several courses (and where I have also had students of strong evangelical beliefs). Cambridge is sometimes nicknamed the Bible Belt of East Anglia, but it is also a place that proves that intellectual endeavor of the highest order and evangelicalism are firmly compatible, so that to live in such a place is a rare privilege.

I should say that the views expressed in this book are my own, and the appearance of people in these acknowledgments does not mean that they would agree with all that is written here.

One

Some Core Evangelical Beliefs

Let's take what many Christians call a *basis of faith* to describe what specifically *evangelical* Christians believe. I have deliberately chosen to use an interdenominational statement of faith , since many such bases of faith are peculiar to a particular group. In other words, each denomination has its own individual sets of doctrine (as the Baptist joke goes, you can baptize people your way, and we will do it God's way), whereas what follows is something believed in by evangelical Christians across all kinds of divergent groups: Baptist, Methodist, Presbyterian, Lutheran, and many other Protestant groups.

I have chosen the doctrinal faith basis of the International Fellowship of Evangelical Students, a body which, as we shall see in chapter 3, has members in over 152 countries and is therefore multicultural and supranational; it has a presence on every continent, and is not restricted to just one country, as is the case with many Protestant denominations.[1]

The central truths, as revealed in Scripture, include:

1. The unity of the Father, Son, and Holy Spirit in the Godhead. This is what we call the doctrine of the Trinity, and it is one of the oldest and most distinctive Christian beliefs. It is vital because who Jesus is, what he came to do, and what he accomplished is at the heart of the Christian message—the *evangel*, or good news, from which the term *evangelical*, someone who both believes in and proclaims the *evangel*, gets its name. Jesus was no mere good man—he was and still is God the Son, part of the Trinity itself.

2. The sovereignty of God in creation, revelation, redemption, and final judgment. God is in charge, and we are all beholden to him. This is vital in all kinds of different ways; for example, it is why supporting the need for a clean environment is part and parcel of being a responsible Christian, since the Bible teaches that we are the stewards God mandated to look after his creation properly. In Britain Christians of all the different political persuasions support environmental responsibility, although, of course, there are diverse opinions on how this should best be implemented. The same is increasingly true in the United States as well as in what I will refer to in this book as the Two-thirds World, that is, Asia, Africa, and Latin America, where most of the human race is living. This part of the statement is wide-ranging in its application.

But of course this part of the statement is also about that taboo word *judgment*. Our noncondemnatory, touchy-feely modern world doesn't like such words. We cannot avoid it though—our natural condition is to be in rebellion against God, and this puts us under his condemnation. Thankfully, God provides a way of redemption, of someone else taking our just punishment, and this way, the Christian message says, is Jesus Christ, God the Son, taking the punishment we deserve on the cross. Needless to say, judgment is not a popular doctrine! Countless people have tried to water it down over the centuries and continue to do so today. But as the word *sovereign* implies, it is God who is King, not us. This goes inherently against the me-decade mentality of early twenty-first-century life. But while God is a God of justice, he is also a God of mercy—redemption and judgment are inexorably linked, as we shall see as this statement unfolds.

3. The divine inspiration and entire trustworthiness of Holy Scripture, as originally given, and its supreme authority in all matters of faith and conduct. This doctrine, which goes back to the Reformation doctrine of *sola scriptura* (Scripture alone) is what the twentieth-century writer and thinker Francis Schaeffer described in 1974 as the "watershed of evangelicalism." It is, one might say, the doctrinal belief that separates evangelicals from other forms of Protestantism today in the same way that, historically speaking, it divided all Protestants after the sixteenth-century Reformation from the dogmas of the Catholic Church. This doctrine states simply that the Bible and not any subsequent tradition is the basis for what we as Christians should believe—that what we read in the Scriptures was inspired by God and is therefore theologically both true and unchangeable, what Schaeffer liked to describe as *true truth*. In other words, why do we believe what we believe? On what basis do we believe it? Or to use that well-worn university jargon phrase, what determines what is normative for Christian belief?

This is not a popular doctrine today either! It is perhaps the most provocative of specifically evangelical beliefs, since the Roman Catholic Church teaches that its own authority is equal to that of the Bible (one of the key disputes it had with the Protestant Reformers, who disagreed strongly) and post-nineteenth-century theological liberals in the Protestant churches think that human reason is either equal to or supersedes the ancient foundational texts of the Christian church, which is what the Bible claims to be.

4. The universal sinfulness and guilt of all people since the fall, rendering them subject to God's wrath and condemnation. People often think that Christians consider themselves better than others. But it should be the exact opposite: one of the key doctrines of evangelicalism has the wonderful—if slightly antique—name of *total depravity*. Absolutely all people are sinners, however nice and kind they may be, however often they help little old ladies across the road, remember to give to charity, and pay their taxes. As the Old Testament book of Isaiah reminds us, even our most righteous deeds are filth. One of the things that people often forget about Jesus is the regularity with which he clearly taught about hell and how we are all due to go there unless we repent of our sins before God. However good we are, all that goodness will and can never get us to heaven. Christians should be known for *not* thinking highly of themselves.

Needless to say, total depravity is not a doctrine that makes evangelicals at all popular, since we are those who proclaim it the most. It is not just the politically correct who dislike this facet of evangelical Christian faith, but also those whose Christianity is one of good works, friendliness, occasional attendance at church, and the belief that being English or a patriotic American is probably enough to convince God that we are splendid folk who deserve a place in heaven. However, there is no escaping it: it is the clear and plain teaching of Scripture and a repeated motif throughout the New Testament, from beginning to end.

For Scripture says is that we are *innately* sinful, regardless of how otherwise decent and honorable we might think ourselves to be. Not only that, we are by nature sinners and rebels against God himself. It is this, as much as any specific sin that we commit, that literally damns us if we are not redeemed. This is why the Ten Commandments start not with coveting our neighbor's ox, but with our relationship with God himself. Without Jesus Christ true worship is impossible, since by nature we always put ourselves first and not God.

So all of us are sinners—it is part of our DNA. Evangelicals realize this about themselves: we know we are not good enough, that we ourselves are sinners, and that we need to daily thank God for our salvation in Jesus Christ.

5. Redemption from the guilt, penalty, dominion, and pollution of sin, solely through the sacrificial death (as our representative and substitute) of the Lord Jesus Christ, the incarnate Son of God. This too is a doctrine that in our age makes evangelical Christians far from popular, for if ever there were a teaching contrary to the pluralistic teachings of our secular, postmodern age, this is it! There is only one way to God, and that is through the sacrificial death of Jesus upon the cross.

Pluralism, and the absence of absolute truth, is intrinsic to our age, even among people who have never heard of postmodernism and would have no idea that they actually believed many of its core tenets. The notion that there are many paths to God, that we can all choose our own, and that all of them are valid is at the heart of the pluralistic twenty-first century. To reject this is to be seen as bigoted, prejudiced, narrow-minded, and many other unfavorable epithets besides. Believing that Jesus is the only way to God is deeply unfashionable in an era in which people think such beliefs went out with the Stone Age.

Many nonevangelical Christians also have pluralistic beliefs; the idea that Buddhism, Islam, and what one might describe as nonjudgmental Christianity are all equally valid options is a key tenet of faith in many churches, cathedrals, and divinity faculties around the world.

Yet time and time again the New Testament firmly rejects such notions, however attractive and nice-sounding they may be to the modern mind. Salvation—reconciliation with God, forgiveness of sins, eternal life—are available through Jesus *and through Jesus alone*. You can't get saved through Buddha, Muhammad, being nice to your aged grandmother, or anything else that we might think of. And it goes without saying that the very notion that we need to be saved at all is also incompatible with the modern zeitgeist.

In fact, the very idea of salvation is based upon the notion of *judgment*—that we are objectively in the wrong and that we need to be saved from the just punishment for our rebellion against God. Judgment even in a secular sense of judging criminals is now increasingly passé, with perpetrators being seen as sick rather than bad and in many senses as much victims of their circumstances as those against whom the crimes have been committed. So the idea that *all* of us are guilty and deserving of punishment by a God entitled to judge us is even more incomprehensible to the twenty-first century secular mind than it was to those of our great-grandparents in another era. Yet as Jesus himself made clear, judgment is very real and facing each and every one of us!

So we evangelicals do not go out expecting to be popular!

But it is interesting, is it not, that of the different expressions of Christianity in Britain and the United States today, it is the evangelical version to which so many turn, even though what evangelicals teach and believe is so resolutely countercultural in the profound sense of that term? And globally, in the Two-thirds World where the vast majority of people live today, it is evangelical Christianity that is growing like never before, especially now that it is seen not as a Western product, but as a system of doctrine authentically multiethnic, multicultural, and genuinely global. Evangelical Christianity tells it as it is, biblically speaking, however unfashionable that might be in pluralistic circles today.

6. The bodily resurrection of the Lord Jesus Christ from the dead and his ascension to the right hand of God the Father. Christianity is based upon facts rather than fantasies and fairy tales. This is something that the writers of the different parts of the New Testament wanted their readers to understand(just look, for example, at the beginning of Luke's Gospel).

A few years back I was at a talk for Christians in Science, a body of evangelical Christians working in science faculties throughout the universities of Britain. The speaker reminded the Cambridge audience that people regarded belief in the resurrection as weird even back in the first century, and that to claim that a proof of Christianity was that, as Paul argued in his epistles, Jesus rose from the dead would be regarded as eccentric by a first-century Roman audience just as it would be by a secular one in the twenty-first. We tend to think that folk two thousand years ago believed all sorts of strange things, but in fact—and certainly in sophisticated circles—their *lack* of belief in such things was as strong as it is now.

Christianity, the Bible and the early church proclaimed, was not based upon fables *but upon facts.* It is a fact that we are all sinners in need of reconciliation with God through Jesus Christ, and it is a fact that God accepted the sacrifice of Jesus on our behalf by raising him from the dead—just as the New Testament describes.

What we call *apologetics*, the defense of a reasonable and authentic Christian faith, is, in today's touchy-feely society, sadly no longer fashionable. But evangelicals are those who believe our faith is founded on reality and not upon warm-fuzzies, however glowing inside such things might make us. Remember, Christianity is *true truth*.

7. The presence and power of the Holy Spirit in the work of regeneration. The Holy Spirit is the third member of the Trinity, and, evangelicals believe, plays a key role in someone becoming a Christian, which is what is meant by the technical term *regeneration* (literally *rebirth*, or, to use the more well-known phrase, "born-again"). The key Christian distinctive, and one that evangelicals stress, especially those in the Reformed tradition, is that *God takes the initiative*. The Holy Spirit works in us to convict us that we are sinners who need the salvation that only Jesus Christ can provide, and this in turn leads us to be open to God's offer of salvation through the cross. We do not become Christians unaided, since naturally speaking we are against God and all his demands upon us. And, when we are converted—born again—the Holy Spirit continues to dwell in us, helping us to pray, to understand things from a spiritual perspective, and to live lives in accordance with the will of God.

8. The justification of the sinner by the grace of God through faith alone. This is the great Reformation doctrine known in the sixteenth century to Martin Luther, John Calvin, John Knox, and Thomas Cranmer as *sola fide*, by faith alone. It is at the heart of what makes Protestants of all descriptions, not just evangelicals, quite different from both Roman Catholicism and Eastern Orthodoxy. This is a critical evangelical perspective, since it is not just Catholic teaching that emphasizes the importance of works, to use the technical term, or good deeds, but much of mainstream society and what we might call nominal Protestantism (of the "I am a decent Briton/American whose kind deeds will get me to heaven" variety). No, we only get to heaven and are reconciled with God through faith in the finished and complete work of Christ on our behalf, since nothing that we can ever do or say for ourselves is good enough to get us there. Only Jesus saves, and only our faith in that saving action *justifies* us, or declares sinners like us righteous in the eyes of God. Jesus has taken the punishment that is our due, and without that we are judicially guilty and lost.

9. The indwelling and work of the Holy Spirit in the believer. All evangelicals hold to this regardless of their views on much-debated issues such as the continued existence of the so-called "sign gifts," such as speaking in tongues, miraculous healing, prophecy, and issues of that nature. Note that the IFES basis of faith does not refer to matters such as "baptism with the Holy Spirit," which evangelical charismatics in mainstream denominations and Pentecostal evangelicals believe is a special experience of the Holy Spirit that takes place after conversion, and is usually indicated by speaking in what they regard as a heavenly language, or "tongues." Some sociologists of religion prefer, for this reason, to separate Pentecostals from evangelicals both in the United States and the United Kingdom and, above all, in the Two-thirds World, where Pentecostalism is the form of Christianity growing by far the largest in terms of sheer numbers. But IFES does not do this nor, I think, should we. For the *core* faith and beliefs of many Pentecostal denominations are thoroughly evangelical in their nature, and millions of Pentecostal students worldwide would most emphatically identify themselves as evangelical and as some of the most active members today of IFES.

While there is huge scope for divergence on some issues, I would agree with one of the founders of Protestantism in the sixteenth century, Martin Luther, who felt that there were matters *essential* to the faith—the kind of things we are looking at in this chapter—and what he described as matters *indifferent*, issues upon which there are legitimate differences of opinion, but which are, so to speak, within the family. In his day one of the hot potato issues was the nature of the communion service (still a bone of contention today) and that of the way in which the church should be run, again an issue as resonant in the twenty-first century as in the sixteenth. This is not to say that many evangelicals would find some of their fellow-evangelicals in Pentecostal denominations or in the charismatic wing of existing denominations unusual, but then evangelical Pentecostals would probably wonder why the rest of us don't grasp the Bible's clear teaching—as they would see it—in the way that they do!

But *all* evangelicals, of all myriad persuasions on this issue, believe that we have the Holy Spirit in us from conversion, from when we first become a Christian believer, and as the IFES statement is inclusive of all evangelicals, it naturally emphasizes what we all believe in common, without getting into doctrinal disputes within the family.

10. The one holy universal church, which is the body of Christ and to which all true believers belong. This is how true Christians see the church. The outside world sees one large Roman Catholic group, or, in some countries, the official Orthodox Church, and then globally hundreds (probably thousands) of diverse Protestant denominations, all of which seem to spend as much time disagreeing with each other as anything else. But this part of the doctrinal basis makes it very clear—*there is only one Christian church.* We will look at this in more detail elsewhere as it is greatly perplexing to outsiders, but the doctrine is clear: whatever manmade differences might exist (Protestant/ Catholic, or Baptist/Methodist, or many Presbyterian or Pentecostal denominations), all true believing Christians are, from God's point of view, his people in a single body of believers. Denominations are part of the lives of most evangelicals, but their ultimate loyalty does, or certainly should, cross denominational boundaries, since what unites us as evangelicals is far more important than what divides us as Episcopalians, Presbyterians, Methodists, Baptists, Pentecostals, or whatever manmade divisions may exist.

11. The expectation of the personal return of the Lord Jesus Christ. Jesus is coming back! But note what this part of the doctrinal basis does and *does not* say. All evangelicals believe Jesus is going to return, to finish history, to hold the last judgment, and to inaugurate a new heaven and a new earth. But this statement does not say *how* this will be accomplished. The reason is simple—within evangelical Christianity, there are scores of divergent views on what Christians describe as *eschatology*, the study of the second coming of Jesus Christ at the end of time. Even the famous Left Behind series, which has sold millions of copies, is only one interpretation even within a much wider belief system held by some evangelicals known as premillennialism. And, to give another North American example, the Puritans and the founding fathers had quite another set of beliefs about the return of Christ altogether. But the key thing is this: all evangelicals expect Christ's personal return even if they disagree on the details. This is one of the reasons I have chosen the particular interdenominational, multicultural, and international but thoroughly evangelical statement of faith at which we are looking, because if evangelicals in the United States or in Britain disagree about some of these specific details, so do all evangelical Christians across the globe. But remember—it is the details on which they differ, like the issues of baptism or church government, not the basic doctrine that Jesus is coming back. We will look at this issue again later in the book.

Nonessentials

Let us note one important thing: what we have examined above are the core beliefs of evangelicals around the world, no matter their denominational stripe. These are the central doctrines that evangelicals have in common with each other, even if they are not in agreement on anything else!

I have already mentioned one issue in which some are not in agreement: what Pentecostals and charismatic Christians within mainstream denominations call the gifts of the Holy Spirit. Personally, I have no problem with someone being evangelical and, say, a charismatic Anglican or a member of an Assemblies of God church, and indeed in many countries, such people are the heart of the evangelical community. Sadly there are some holdouts among what we call cessationists, those who believe that the miraculous sign gifts, such as speaking in tongues or miraculous healing, have ceased, and that therefore those who believe such gifts exist today cannot be evangelicals in the proper sense.

Likewise, as we shall see in the chapter on the end times, there are also those, mainly in the United States but some outside it as well, who insist that only those with their particular form of eschatology are *truly* evangelical.

I think that this is all a great shame. To reverse some Bing Crosby song lyrics, such folk are accentuating the negative and not the positive. Nonetheless, that there are those who would tighten the criteria for admission into "evangelicalism" does show one thing about us: we can be an argumentative people! But that, I would argue, is the underside of the positive thing about evangelicals: *we do actually believe something*. Indeed, we are a people defined by our beliefs, and that is what distinguishes us in our twenty-first-century postmodern times: we still hold firm to a belief system when so many others regard belief in anything as something eccentric. Even as far back as the eighteenth century the aristocracy in Britain and the higher reaches of the established church disliked evangelicals as *enthusiasts*, the kind of people who were actually serious about their beliefs and were excited by them. That is still the case today, which is why evangelicals are still regarded as somewhat over-the-top by those in our contemporary culture for whom a postmodern worldview and sense of detachment, as well as the wish not only to be cool but to be *seen* to be cool is considered to be the height of good manners. (Needless to say, challenge the inner beliefs of such people, and they become very hot and not at all cool!)

In the next chapter we will look at the basic vision statement of the church my wife and I attend in Cambridge, England, because it is typical, despite being both English and in a university town, of many evangelical churches in the United Kingdom, the United States, and around the world. One of the criticisms that could be made against it is just the same kind made by those eighteenth-century grandees: *your church is very enthusiastic.*

It is true that some evangelical churches are so doctrinally rigid that, to use a common expression, they could be called the *frozen chosen.* But one thing that normally characterizes evangelical churches is that they want to welcome outsiders and to share their faith with nonbelievers. In a postmodern age in which any kind of absolute belief is taboo (except for *that* notion, of course), this is no longer acceptable. And, as we shall see elsewhere in this book, it is thus significant that it is in the Two-thirds World where belief is still acceptable and evangelical Christianity is growing the fastest.

One Body

Apart from a small grouping of evangelical Catholics—whose existence as such is not always accepted by other evangelicals—evangelicalism is a product, as we shall see, of the great Protestant Reformation of the sixteenth century, the returning to biblical roots of the Christian faith. There is one Roman Catholic Church; there are hundreds if not thousands of Protestant denominations, of all bewildering beliefs and practices. So it is tempting to say there are many kinds of evangelicalism; there are plenty of sociologists of religion who would split Pentecostalism off as something quite different from historic evangelicalism as it has developed over the centuries.

Chapter 4 covers church history, and I have written another whole work on the subject: *Church History: A Crash Course for the Curious.*[2] But because the existence of so many Protestant denominations is an issue that puzzles bewildered outsiders and that the secular media often get very wrong, we need to examine it here both historically and doctrinally. I would argue that evangelical Christianity is, in essence, far more united than it is disunited, and that it is at its core as much one movement as even the Catholic Church, united by its central tenets of belief as much as the Catholics are united as one body under the pope.

Protestant Christianity, by its very historic definition, has no pope. The Bible, in theory, unites Protestant Christians, and in both theory and practice it is at the heart of evangelical Christianity. Evangelicals are Bible people, since they believe that God's Word, the Scriptures, Old and New Testaments, define *what* we believe and *why*.

So how do they differ from other Protestants and from Roman Catholics (and the various versions of Orthodoxy)? Let us look at that first, and then at why there seem to be such a plethora of denominations within Protestantism, and whether or not that actually matters.

Back when British prime ministers still directly appointed bishops (they now just consult), television political comedies often made the joke that belief in God was not a prerequisite for the appointment! By and large, while only a very few clergy really are atheist or agnostic, many of the nonevangelical clergy in not just the Church of England but also in plenty of other older denominations have not believed in much of the Bible for a very long time—not just since the rise of German critical theology in the nineteenth century, which is often blamed, but since even the eighteenth century, when many a bishop had long ceased to take the Bible seriously.

That was not the case with the evangelicals of the Great Awakening— as we shall see in future chapters—nor is it the case with evangelicals today. We still remain people who actually read and hold true to the Scriptures of the first century. Truth, evangelicals believe, does not change. Two plus two equaled four in first century Palestine or Rome, and it still does today. The human condition and the reality of sin has not changed either, as the eminent Welsh twentieth-century preacher, Martyn Lloyd-Jones, proclaimed in the sermons published in book form as *The Cross*.[3] Certainly we live longer, we have become technically more sophisticated—I am using computer technology to write this and to send it electronically that did not even exist fifteen years ago—but *as humans we remain the same*.

This, therefore, is the major divergence between evangelicals and other Protestants: we still hold to those two Reformation truths of *sola fide* and *sola scriptura*, which, as one of evangelicalism's best-known advocates, John Stott, has argued, is no more or less than mainstream Christianity, the beliefs of the Christians of the first century when the faith began.

Needless to say, those not of evangelical persuasion would disagree! We often read of the "old mainstream denominations" in the United States, usually with the word "decline" not far away, as if they were the mainstream and evangelicalism were some new and aberrant form of belief. But if one looks at what the so-called mainstream churches believe, they are more significant for what they no longer believe than what they still do.

In this they are not alone—Roman Catholicism is nowhere near as uniform in belief as its adherents would want to have us suppose. Certainly the present pope (like his predecessor) is on the conservative side of the doctrinal debates of our time. But it is often their fellow Catholics who are most outraged by some or another papal pronouncement, especially Catholics in the West. Liberal theology has not entered Protestantism only, but Catholicism as well, as the works of many an American or British Catholic reveal. And in that sense, therefore, one could argue legitimately that liberal Catholics and liberal Protestants have more in common with each other than they do with more conservative believers within their own nominal camps. Increasingly, as the influential American magazine *First Things* (one read by many Catholics and evangelicals) has suggested, "Protestant versus Catholic" is no longer as meaningful a distinction as once existed, since liberals in both camps are now more in line with secular modernity and thus with nonbelievers. (Traditional Catholics will reject my description of Roman Catholicism as a denomination, since they believe that truth lies solely with them. But then as an evangelical, I would argue what I do!)

Evangelical Christianity is thus distinct both from liberal Protestantism and from its Catholic equivalent in what it regards as the source of authority and the reasons for belief.

It also differs, as Protestant, from historic Catholicism. *Sola scriptura* meant that no priest, let alone a pope, had the right to interpret Scripture in a way that was binding upon all believers. Similarly, the Protestant rediscovery of the *priesthood of all believers* (which, by a nice irony, is a teaching found in the Bible chiefly in Peter's first epistle, the apostle that Catholics believe was the first pope) means that there is no need for an intermediary priesthood between God and ordinary Christians.[4] (We will see more about this when we look at a specific evangelical church in chap. 2.)

By the time of the Reformation, the teaching of the Catholic Church was that *tradition was equal in authority to Scripture.* In Protestantism, and thus in evangelical Christianity, only Scripture determines doctrine.

This means, for example, that specifically Catholic doctrines, such as those on Mary or on the existence of a place such as Purgatory, find no place in any kind of Protestantism. Protestants believe, for instance, that Mary married Joseph after Christ's birth and had other children by him (as the Bible also suggests; Luke 8:19) and that while Mary is someone to be much revered, she nonetheless plays no role in the process of salvation. We pray to Jesus alone, not to his mother. As for Purgatory, to Protestants no such place exists, and therefore the initials on many a Catholic grave—*RIP* (*requiescat in pace*, rest in peace)—do not apply, since true believers go straight to heaven upon their death. Similarly there are considerable differences between Protestants and historic Catholics on what we believe actually happens at the communion service, or Eucharist.

However, without need of the pope or an intermediary priesthood between God and his people, evangelicals often face a downside in terms of actual practice.

Think of communion, for instance. No Protestant believes that Christ is *literally* present in the bread and wine. But within a few years of the dawn of the Reformation in 1517, Protestants were already disagreeing among themselves, often vehemently, about what communion was all about. Lutherans argued that while Christ was not *physically* present he was certainly *symbolically* present in a special way, while the followers of the Swiss theologian, Zwingli, believed that communion was a commemoration and that the Lutheran view was too similar to the Catholic doctrine for comfort.

Matters indifferent are at the very heart of Protestantism precisely because of the liberty of conscience it gives to individual believers to interpret God's Word for themselves, through the Holy Spirit working in the hearts and minds of every Christian.

This, for example, is why Baptists have their particular set of interpretations of what baptism is all about in the New Testament, and Presbyterians and Anglicans quite another. It is why some Protestant churches have bishops (including many of the newer African-originated denominations, not just the Church of England), and some, such as the Plymouth Brethren, have no ordained ministers at all. It is also why the Lutherans in Scandinavia still have close ties to the state, whereas in the United States some independent churches are not members of any denomination at all.

But does all this matter? I would argue it is actually rather unimportant, and that in so saying I am being a classic evangelical.

For this is, in many ways, a defining feature of what *evangelical* Christians are like: they have far more in common with each other than they do of people to whom they might be linked by denominational ties, as we shall see in depth in chapter 2. For a Baptist evangelical, who baptizes one way, has, in reality, far more in common with a Presbyterian evangelical who does it another. This has led to evangelicals getting in trouble from time to time with their own denominations, and one could say with good cause, because at the deepest doctrinal level, the accusation that being evangelical is a higher loyalty than being part of a denomination is true. What unites an evangelical Baptist to an evangelical Methodist makes the unity that, say, all Baptists have with each other *less* important than what divides Baptists and Methodists. Evangelicals are putting doctrinal unity ahead of denominational distinctives.

This is what led some evangelicals in the 1960s to wonder why they could not simply unite with one another and stop being in the same denominational groups as those who, for example, denied the divinity of Christ, a key evangelical belief. Many splits did then occur, both in

29

England and in the United States, when many British evangelicals came together in a denomination called the FIEC (Fellowship of Independent Evangelical Churches) and when many American Presbyterians left the Presbyterian Church of the USA (PCUSA) to form the Presbyterian Church of America (PCA).

Many other evangelicals remained within their denominational groups, most notably the evangelical Anglicans. These evangelicals are in the majority in terms of the denomination *worldwide*, with most Anglicans (or Episcopalians, to use the American term) in places such as Nigeria or Latin America being strongly evangelical, but the state Church of England still has a mainly nonevangelical hierarchy in Britain, and evangelicals are a small minority in the Episcopal church in the United States.

So the jury is still out on whether evangelicals should leave their denominational groups.

Interdenominational Groups

Another thing for which evangelicals are well known is parachurch interdenominational groups—of which, once again, IFES is an exemplar. IFES began after the Second World War, when students from around the world, from China to the recently defeated Germany met together in war-torn Europe in evangelical unity. They put behind them the horrors of the past six years to set up an international organization that linked evangelical students regardless of denomination or nationality, to further a deeper understanding of God's Word, and to evangelize their fellow students. The leader of this group and its first chairman, Dr. D. Martyn Lloyd-Jones, was a Welsh physician turned preacher; he would be associated both with this movement and with the intellectual postwar resurgence in global evangelicalism for the next thirty-five years.

What was significant about IFES is that it was not Western-led. Its general secretaries, for example, have included a Chinese, and the current leader is from Ivory Coast. The founding of IFES was not, in other words, a case of missionaries from the West going out to bring Christianity to those in the Two-thirds World. Since in 1945 Britain and France still ruled vast areas of the globe, including most of Africa, this was in itself an unusual move. But as those early IFES pioneers realized, the best way, for example, to reach students in India or Brazil was to send out other students from India or Brazil. This was soon to become more important than they knew, because within three years of their first meeting, China, which had the biggest delegation in 1946, became Communist, and the Iron Curtain fell on other member nations, such as Hungary. Western missions became illegal in such nations, and so the only way the Christian message could be heard in campuses from Beijing to Moscow to Budapest was for brave students living there already to share the message, however dangerously, with others.

Today the strongest IFES movements are often those outside of the West, in what is now the majority part of the Christian world, with Western Europe becoming increasingly secular. Now students from Africa or South America are coming to evangelize us in the West!

There are plenty of other examples of parachurch organizations that are both evangelical and multidenominational. Many student campuses in Britain and the United States have, for example, a Christian Union or an InterVarsity chapter, and it is interesting to reflect that on several British campuses, the University of Exeter being a recent example, avowedly secular student unions have been trying, without legal success so far, to get Christians banned from meeting on campus. *This is not in a Communist country, but in Britain*, a nation with an established church.

Relief agencies, such as World Vision in the United States or Tear Fund in the United Kingdom, also fit into this pattern of evangelicals coming together to bring, in this case, relief and development aid to Two-thirds World countries.

Likewise, many interdenominational mission agencies exist. Some, such as the Overseas Missionary Fellowship (OMF), of nineteenth-century vintage and now in the twenty-first century, have missionaries not just from traditional sending countries, such as the United States and Britain, but now increasingly from former host countries, such as Korea, with Asian evangelicals evangelizing fellow Asians.

The OMF is interesting as it shows that what was done well over a century ago has had massive fruit decades later. OMF was once the China Inland Mission, a pioneering evangelical missionary organization

31

founded by a Briton, Hudson Taylor. It was interdenominational from the start and also international, with American as well as British missionaries going out to China. Its missionaries were, significantly, urged to wear Chinese clothes and to present the gospel in its own right and not as something that was part of the West. Then in 1951, in what was called the Reluctant Exodus, all the Western missionaries were expelled.

Everyone waited to see what would happen next. Some of the other mission agencies had spotted a phenomenon known as "Rice Christians," where people in China would profess Christianity to gain access to the physical benefits that the missionaries brought. But after 1951, being a Chinese Christian could increasingly cost you your life! Certainly many Christians were imprisoned, and during the horrors of the Great Proletarian Cultural Revolution, thousands of Christians died alongside those countless others who suffered during that decade of madness under Chairman Mao.

Then in 1976 the Bamboo Curtain began to lift. I myself was able to go to China not long thereafter, both to see Chinese friends who had studied in London but also to see one of the original IFES Chinese students, now an elderly man, who had been imprisoned for a long time during the Cultural Revolution but had been released and rehabilitated.

What was astonishing (and what we all now know), is that the church, far from being wiped out, had actually grown! Two million Christians in 1951 had grown, according to CIA and United States Commission on International Religious Freedom reports, to as much as *eighty million or more*![5] This is more than a forty-fold increase, and what is especially significant is that the growth took place with the Western missionaries expelled and with the most savage and brutal persecution imaginable. What was also interesting is that many of the areas where the church in China was strongest in 1976, thirty years after the Reluctant Exodus, were those parts of the country where the OMF had been active pre-1951. So all the hard work, health sacrifices, and more besides of the China Inland Mission workers over a hundred-year period—called China's Open Door—had reaped a spiritual harvest far larger than any of them could ever have imagined.

There are, it should be said, plenty of excellent denominational groups and missionary societies. One of the reasons why South Korea is so strongly Christian today—perhaps 50 percent or even more—is because of the faithful work of American Presbyterians in decades gone by. Likewise, the work of the evangelical Anglican missionaries in Latin America has helped to turn much of that continent Protestant, with many Episcopalian churches in the United States now coming under the spiritual oversight of the presiding bishop of the Southern Cone. Many a Southern Baptist missionary is revered around the world, such as Lottie Moon from Virginia, who is still remembered in China today, long after her death. Lutherans carry out essential relief work all over Africa. Campus ministries such as Agape, the student work of the Assemblies of God, and the Reformed University Fellowship, the similar ministry of the PCA, often draw students to their meetings who are not from their particular denominations. (And from Charlottesville to Cambridge, a free lunch will bring students regardless of ecclesiastical background.)

But, by and large, the experience at college, or on a short-term mission trip over a long summer break, or of working with fellow evangelicals across denominational divides usually creates a mindset in young evangelicals that lasts a lifetime. What matters are the evangelical core beliefs that we hold as well as a common sense of purpose in evangelism, rather than those differences that denominations tend to highlight. Baptist, Anglican, Methodist, and Pentecostal students gather together, study God's Word together, and evangelize the campus together—and who baptizes people with which particular method matters less and less.

This does not mean that to evangelicals, individually or corporately, such things cease to matter altogether. We still have our particular views on different issues, such as church government and the gifts of the Holy Spirit. Some evangelicals prefer calm, softer music, whereas others need it at ear-blasting full volume! We are not always comfortable with the worship style of each other's churches or of the different lengths of sermons. Cultural differences also exist, with emphases in one part of the world perhaps being different from those in others.

But, above all, we are still *all evangelicals*, with the strong distinctive beliefs that bind us together, which we have explored in this chapter. In future chapters we will see how evangelicals developed, how some particular evangelical churches function, and how evangelicalism is now a global phenomenon, with its heartland no longer in the West but in the Two-thirds World, in Africa, Asia, and Latin America.

A Typical Evangelical Church's Vision Statement

These days we are all used to our employers having something called a "vision statement": what the company (or school, or agency, or whatever yours is called) does and why it does it. Often this is customer-oriented, so that the great buying public out there can see that your product, educational establishment, or charity is *the* best possible for a person to have, as well as to remind us what it is that we do.

Christian mission statements are different because Christians are not, in the consumer sense, touting for customers—or at least not in the sense that we believe all products are equal and that the only difference between ours and that of our competitors is one of quality. Evangelicals are, as we saw in chapter 1, people who believe in the *uniqueness* of the Christian message, rather than Christianity being somewhat improved over its, say, secular materialist or Buddhist rivals.

But all that said, mission statements are still most helpful, both to remind members of a particular congregation why they are here and to let outsiders—whether Christians coming for the first time to our town or non-Christians visiting with a Christian friend—know who we are and what we do.

St. Andrew the Great's Vision Statement

Let us examine the vision statement of the church I know best: the one that my wife and I attend in Cambridge, St. Andrew the Great, or, strictly speaking, the parish of The Holy Sepulchre with St. Andrew the Great. (We will later look at an American vision statement, one developed by a local church that deliberately sets out to be a role model for many congregations, not just its own.)

I think it's important to look at this particular vision statement because outsiders often think of evangelical congregations as strange, "happy-clappy" churches not linked to any mainstream church group of which they have ever heard, who do weird things in unusual places and are thus rather scary—and who, in the case of those in the United Kingdom, *are definitely not British.* The reality is that in Britain, as in South America and in large parts of Africa such as Nigeria or Uganda, it is possible to be both thoroughly and unashamedly evangelical *and* part of a church that has existed for hundreds of years or more. (And, as we shall see, "happy-clappy" is a term that is widely misunderstood, relating to *styles* of worship rather than to a particular church's core beliefs, which can be as solidly evangelical as the more worship-conservative Baptist church down the road.)

In one sense, St. Andrew the Great is a church whose vision has changed over time, and in our case, *lots* of time, since we are over nine hundred years old! It would have been Catholic for the first half of its existence, then changing to Protestant with the advent of the Reformation in the 1530s.

Today we are a congregation in one of the biggest university towns in Britain. As Anglia Ruskin University likes to remind people, there are in fact two universities in Cambridge, not just the more famous one (Cambridge University itself). But there are also thousands of students in the city who are not studying at either university; these are language students attending one of the many English teaching establishments, usually studying to earn the Cambridge Certificate in the English Language. We therefore have a huge student body in our congregation, with hundreds attending each week. This in itself is significant, demonstrating that evangelical Christianity is the expression of Protestant faith that appeals to the majority of students making some kind of outward Christian profession of faith. This is true of people from all over the globe, since our student congregation and that of theologically similar churches in Cambridge is highly international.

Because of the University of Cambridge, we are also the Palo Alto of Europe. What used to be called the "Cambridge effect" has sparked the development of hundreds of high technology companies, often spun off from Nobel Prize winning university research (one of Cambridge's institutions has as many Nobel laureates as France). Some of these companies are now major players in their own right. Cambridge is surrounded by flat fenland (some of which used to be below sea level), so we are now nicknamed "Silicon Fen." As a result Cambridge is filled with bright young professionals, some of whom are there just for a few years before being poached to work elsewhere, and others for whom Cambridge is a lifetime commitment. The demographics of our church reflect this as well, having an enormous group of people in their twenties and thirties, many initially single, and from all over the world. Significantly, the bulk of these people are scientists, which again disproves a twenty-first-century myth that Christianity (its evangelical wing in particular) has nothing to say to modern individuals in a scientific age.

There are a few congregants who are neither students nor thirty-something scientists, otherwise my wife (who is a musician) would truly stand out! We would probably be more typical in towns outside of Cambridge, with no university or significant technology/medical employer, but we can leave all that aside for now.

Our church is therefore:

- Ancient—founded well over nine hundred years ago.
- Anglican—part of the Church of England.
- Evangelical—having a theological identity that is not just denominational.
- In a major university town—welcoming a huge student congregation.

- In one of Europe's main technological centers—having a core of highly qualified scientific professionals.
- International—witnessing an influx of people from all over the world.

What, therefore, is St. Andrew the Great's vision statement?

A Church Committed to the Bible and to Prayer

This first part is *theological* (what we believe).

At the heart of our ministry is teaching the Bible as God's key instrument for proclaiming Jesus Christ as Lord and for building up his followers on earth. Our worship is the offering of our entire lives to God in holiness and service. At our main meetings we aim (1) to encourage each other to feed ourselves on God's Word and to give ourselves to prayer, so that we may worship God better in our lives; and (2) to draw in outsiders without embarrassment.

A Church Committed to a Specific Mission

The second part is what one might describe in theological terms as *missiological*: on whom do we concentrate in particular, given our location? (Think about the term "missiological." We talk about Christian *missionaries* but also about our company's *mission* statement without realizing that we are using the same term.)

It is St. Andrew the Great's special task to serve the university community in which we are placed. There are two aspects of our church ("town" and "gown"), but both depend on one another: by becoming a better "normal" church, we also become a better student church.

A Church Committed to Mature Discipleship for Every Member

What, then, are the results of having this kind of church?

Some people are paid to organize the church's life, but all are ministers of the gospel. So we meet in smaller groups to encourage each other to identify our spiritual gifts and to use them to serve others. All members should have a vision of what God wants them to do with their lives for his own glory. We believe that God means us to grow both individually and as a church, that growth means change, and that change may be painful. We accept the pain of change gladly for the sake of bringing the gospel to our contemporaries.

What do we glean from a church such as St. Andrew the Great? It is:

- Bible-centered and Christ-centered. These are two hallmarks of evangelicalism.
- Target-oriented. It is in a university town and thus geared toward the people in that particular environment; it is outward-looking, a trait of evangelical churches globally.
- Discipleship-centered. This is also a specifically evangelical distinctive, and it can involve pain. St. Andrew the Great is not the consumer-led, warm-fuzzy, me-centered kind of megachurch (well-known not just in the United States but in countries such as Brazil), which is often confused with "evangelical" by the secular media, but which is, in fact, entirely different, as we shall see.

Note one thing: nowhere does the vision statement mention anything *denominational*. There is no reference to the fact that we are, technically speaking, a *Church of England* church, and, in our case, by far the biggest contributor to central diocesan funds in the entire Ely diocese. Some American students studying at Cambridge have been astonished to find out we were Anglican—they thought we must be Baptist!

But this too is a hallmark of evangelicalism—loyalty to the core tenets of biblical, Christ-centered faith matters far more to evangelicals than manmade issues of denominational loyalty. I can see why some of the American students mistook our denominational affiliation; St. Andrew the Great, along with numerous other evangelical Anglican churches, practices believer's baptism by immersion (the church has a large baptismal pool where many traditional churches have their altar). And while this is not strange for an evangelical church, many of which practice believer's baptism by immersion while not being part of a specifically Baptist denomination, to outsiders this is frequently a strange thing to see in an Anglican building!

Lessons from St. Andrew the Great

What can we draw from the fact that a church like St. Andrew the Great is evangelical, especially in a place such as Cambridge?

To begin with, Cambridge is not only the number 1 ranked university in the United Kingdom (I write this as someone who graduated from Oxford—the *other place*—and who has a doctorate from Britain's number 35 ranked university in Norwich), but it is also one of the top ten in the world, along with places such as Harvard and Yale. In the year that I write this, 2009, it is celebrating the two-hundredth anniversary of its most famous alumnus, Charles Darwin, the scientist and founder of evolutionary theory, who while not anti-Christian, was most certainly an agnostic.

Yet Cambridge is also one of the most Christian, and indeed evangelical, cities in the United Kingdom, with its evangelical churches—Anglican, Baptist, Presbyterian, Brethren, and charismatic "house church"—thriving, particularly among students and science graduates. Not only that, but one of the colleges, St. Edmund's, has a research body, the Faraday Institute for Science and Religion, staffed by some of the most revered scientists in the university community. The Institute is designed specifically to prove that science and Christian faith are indeed not only compatible, but are together the only logical way of seeing the universe that God has created.

In other words, all this turns what the sociologists call "secularization theory" completely on its head; as science progresses, and as we discover more, not only is Christianity in general flourishing, but so is its evangelical component. It is the evangelical churches that are bursting at the seams—and with students, defying those who reject theological conservatism and claim that only by a very liberal interpretation of the Scriptures can the gospel be appealing to so-called modern people. It is ironic, is it not, that those "modern people" whom the theologically conservative forms of Christianity were supposed to alienate from the Christian message are *precisely* those people who are becoming born-again evangelical Christians at Cambridge University, and in the twenty-first century.

I do not intend to boast of "success" in the sense of a company boasting of post-Christmas sales. Far from it! The *message* of evangelical

Christianity is the thing that is drawing people, computer experts, molecular biologists, engineers, geologists—and, thank goodness for some of us, the occasional student or graduate in history or music—to believing in the claims of Christ as Savior, proclaimed in the first century just as in the present, two thousand years later.

So on a Sunday morning you will find hundreds of students listening to a sermon on Luke and in the evening scores of young professionals to a sometimes quite complex unfolding of the book of Judges, with an interpretation that would be no different from when the great Charles Simeon first decided to evangelize the university back in the eighteenth century. Simeon's efforts, by the way, eventually gave birth to the Jesus Lane work among Christian students in Cambridge that still exists and is now all over the world.

Scientists, as Richard Dawkins always reminds us, want to know about *truth*. It is historians and English literature specialists, alas, who love to waffle and indulge in postmodern, nothing-is-true-except-that-nothing-is-true woolly relativism. (Although, as the Regius Professor of Modern History at Cambridge reminds us, if all *narratives* and *stories* are equally valid and entitled to respect, then logically speaking we have to give full equality and credence to the truth claims of Nazism, racism, and the Third Reich. Not that we historians always want to credit scientists with superior claims of knowledge, but at least they, as theologian D. A. Carson once said in a Cambridge sermon, *do* believe that there truly is such a thing as *true truth*.)

So it is perhaps not surprising that in the postmodern, relativist, postreligious, secular, materialistic world that is Britain and Western Europe, those who actually do believe that such a thing as truth exists should naturally take very seriously the truth claims of the Christian gospel that evangelical Christianity proclaims, despite the political incorrectness of beliefs in absolute and unique truth. As the American sociologist (and evangelical) James Davison Hunter once told a group of us, "At least Marxists believe in *something*," and, as the continuing appeal of the evangelical wing of Christian faith tells us, so do even the most atheistic of scientists.

So the health of evangelical Christianity in a world-class university city such as Cambridge is not just a tribute to the quality of the after-service coffee or the winsome smile of the parish assistant handing you your service sheet as you enter the church—though a friendly welcome does of course help. It is the *message* as well as the messengers, or, if you like, the *evangel* itself, the good news of Jesus Christ, as well as the evangelicals who proclaim it.

Priesthood of All Believers

You will also notice that St. Andrew the Great is not very hierarchical: as mentioned earlier, some people are paid to organize the church's life, but *all* are ministers of the gospel. This too is something evangelicals emphasize, and, in another context, is one of the reasons why evangelical Christianity is spreading so rapidly in South America. There the growth is at the expense of traditional Catholicism, where the dire shortage of ordained priests (not just caused by the Catholic insistence on celibacy) is causing thousands of Brazilians, Chileans, and others to leave their ancestral Catholicism to turn to laity-friendly Protestantism, since married and single lay people can play a fulfilling role.

Our church does of course have traditional paid clergy—in our case a vicar and two curates—but it also has a dozen or so other staff who are full-time and paid, but are not, in the technical sense of the word, *ordained*. This too is typical for an evangelical church. Because evangelicals believe the Bible, they believe in the New Testament's teaching on the priesthood of all believers. This belief is something that historians have long since realized was one of the most powerful rediscoveries of the sixteenth-century Protestant Reformation.

So while in a technical and formal sense our vicar is ordained, he does not regard himself as a priest different from or superior to other members of the congregation. In an evangelical church there is no separation between *priesthood* and *laity* that you find in Roman Catholic or high church Anglican churches. Our vicar is known simply as "Mark," and, in his case, most emphatically *not* "Father Mark," as he would be in a Roman Catholic or Anglo-Catholic traditional church. This is because in evangelical churches *there is no laity*—to evangelicals all believers are priests.

(It is worth noting here that evangelicals in the Church of England are thus not against the ordination of women, since all Christian women are automatically "ordained" in a sense on conversion, but they do have a debate among themselves on what *authority* a women can legitimately have within the structures of the church. But that debate is on what Scripture says, rather than on what the tradition of the church dictates, something therefore entirely different from the views of Anglo-Catholics within the Anglican communion.)

What we consider *laity* is of crucial importance in any evangelical church, whether Anglican or not. The vicar does not have a particular role as *priest*, since everyone in the congregation are priests. Rather, his role is that of exercising one of the biblical gifts, namely that of pastor/teacher, a gift that is listed in many different places in the New Testament epistles. His principal job is thus to be the senior pastoral figure in the church, and also to concentrate on preaching from the Bible in his capacity as a teacher of God's Word.

Home Group Bible Studies

But the pastor is not the only teacher in the congregation. A phenomenon that often interests non-Christians looking in from the outside is the small group Bible study, or as it is often called these days, the home group.

Home groups consist of ordinary members of the congregation meeting together each week in the home of one of their members. At St. Andrews, these consist of ten to fifteen people, and they are normally geographically based so that people do not have to travel too far to get to the meetings. (My wife and I hosted a Bible study in our own home for nearly fifteen years, and now the one we attend is within walking distance.) No ordained member of the staff is present, and the leaders have regular jobs—a medical doctor, bookseller, computer programmer, academic, and music teacher in the case of our group. The leaders rotate weekly, because in-depth Bible study is quite a time-consuming business when taken seriously, and thus requires a major chunk out of a busy working person's week.

The actual study lasts about forty-five minutes to an hour. Everyone is encouraged to take part and to speak, so that we can have a proper discussion, and it is hoped that everyone has read the assigned Scripture passage ahead of time. This empowering of the "laity" (to put it in ecclesiastical terms) was not only one of the keynotes of the Reformation, when an infallible pope and a Bible in Latin were dropped in favor of the innate authority of Scripture itself and a Bible in your own language, but also of evangelical Christianity today, worldwide. God's Word is what tells us what we believe and how we should live, and the best way to find out what it says is to study it for yourself and in the company of others to encourage you.

Much time—probably another forty-five minutes or so—is spent in prayer. Home group leaders are like subpastors, and with a group of only fifteen or so people, all of whom see each other at least weekly (and usually at church, if they attend services at the same time), effective discipleship is much easier than if a vicar finds himself having to look after the needs of nine hundred people, as would be the case for St. Andrew the Great. Pastoring is as much listening as anything else, and it entails mutual support and sharing of burdens. Praying for one another creates a great sense of mutual empathy, the kind of fellowship of believers to which the Bible refers repeatedly throughout the New Testament.

In our church and in many other evangelical parishes and chapels, home groups often pray for missionaries from their congregation now serving overseas. Ours, for example, has two former members who now serve in training colleges in Kenya and who had previously spent several years in Ethiopia. Other home groups have missionaries serving in countries where Christianity is often persecuted and where the very act of getting together to study the Bible can be illegal. (As I will point out elsewhere, this is a helpful reminder to us that while we in the West might suffer the occasional cutting remark at work or blank stares of incomprehension, we are certainly not undergoing the same treatment that millions of fellow believers face every day, some in countries where Christians are being jailed and put to death.)

Evangelicals in particular, with the majority of them living in the Two-thirds World and not the West, are especially aware of these global issues, and most evangelical churches in Britain make sure that their congregations are kept regularly up-to-date with news from overseas.

Integration of Different Ages

While some evangelical churches have ministries that split people by *age*—and our twenties and thirties ministry among young professionals effectively does this—home groups have people of all different ages, educational backgrounds, and professional careers. Not everyone in my home group went to university, for instance, although Cambridge is a very graduate-inhabited town; some are young with small children and one member is retired. (Our church encourages members of the twenties/thirties group to join home groups if they are likely to become long-term residents of Cambridge; yuppies are often, by definition, creatures of transience.)

This integration of different ages differs from what similar churches in the United States might do, which shows that even English-speaking evangelicals are not always joined at the hip! British evangelical Anglicans are often strongly influenced by Australia rather than by North America, since the international influence of the strongly evangelical Archdiocese of Sydney is widespread. In the United States, evangelical churches often use what sociologists give the ghastly name of *the homogenous unit principle*, namely that like people want to get together with other like people because they feel more comfortable among their own kind.

While cities often do have similar kinds of people living there—one cannot avoid the influence of both the university and of "Silicon Fen" in Cambridge—I think it is true to say that many British evangelicals feel that, biblically speaking, the church is by definition highly diverse. The apostle Paul makes clear in his epistles that Christians are not to distinguish between rich and poor, slave and free, male and female, Jewish and Gentile, and all the other distinctions that we, as humans, create to divide us. What the secular world segregates, we, God's people, the church, bring together.

Therefore, in an evangelical parish church or Baptist chapel, what matters is not your job, educational achievement, or race, but whether you are *in Christ, a new creation* (to use just two biblical terms), with the most important thing being what you are *now*, as a Christian believer.

Home groups mirror this new, Christian way of doing things. This is why the "Mature Discipleship for Every Member" part of our mission statement emphasizes the use of *spiritual* gifts. Your job *outside* the church does not always relate to your status *within* the church, whether in the congregation in general or one's home group in particular.

It is often a cliché, for example, that housebound little old ladies are often the best "prayer warriors" in the congregation, since they can stay in their homes praying eagerly for not only local church and individual needs, but also for the work of Christian missions around the world. I once was in a church where there was just such a little old lady—a British woman who had lived, decades before, in Peru, and who had come back to England in retirement. I can say that the cliché is more often a reality than not.

Spiritual Gifts

The phrase "spiritual gifts" can scare some people witless! For some it immediately brings to mind worshipers barking like dogs (which has happened in some churches in recent years), waving their arms in the air, "speaking in tongues" (which can sound *very* weird to those not used to such phenomena), and much else besides.

While there is a small charismatic minority at St. Andrew the Great, most Sunday worshipers do not raise their hands, and very few actually speak in tongues (and not during the service). One could therefore say that our parish is neutral. We are more than happy for those who do practice the more unusual-looking gifts to practice them at home should they so wish (and in home groups should the other members feel comfortable). We are not cessationist (i.e., teaching that the so-called "sign gifts" ceased in the first century AD), but we are not a "charismatic church" in the sense that most people understand that term either.

However, like many evangelical churches, we *do* believe that most of the gifts still exist, and that they should be actively practiced by everyone. This is not as controversial as it may sound! For while the more exotic gifts, for want of a better term, are still highly contentious— tongues, prophecy, and healing, to name just three—others are not.

For example, *administration* is a biblical gift of the Holy Spirit. Where would any church be without able administrators? In the case of our church and that of countless others around the world, the financial structure to have a full-time paid administrator does not exist. Much, if not most, of the administration has to be done part-time, often during the day by helpful retired parishioners and in the evenings by those with regular nine-to-five jobs. Exercising the spiritual gift of administration is vital for a church's spiritual health!

Our own home group is particularly blessed by those within it who have the biblical gift of *hospitality*. I'm not talking about those who occasionally have close friends around; I'm referring to people who practice hospitality sometimes weekly, for years at a time, and in the case of one wonderful couple in our church, decades at a time. We all like being hospitable from time to time, but the Bible is quite right to see the ability to offer hospitality above and beyond the normal course of friendship as a special gift.

The gift of *pastor,* as we have seen, does not just apply to our vicar. The home group leaders are exercising this spiritual gift at the microlevel, and in a good home group everyone joins in to pastor each other.

Discernment of spiritual issues is not some kind of magic, or should certainly not be seen as that. In one sense all Christians need discernment, because there is so much strange stuff out there these days, but God seems to give it in special measure to some people. Having people with the gift of discernment makes an enormous difference not just to a home group but to a church as a whole.

So we see that there are plenty of spiritual gifts of an unspectacular and noncontroversial kind, and home groups are ideal for seeing who has what and how such gifts can be used, as the Bible insists they must be, for the wider edification of fellow believers in the church.

Thus home groups of nonordained members, all of whom, in the evangelical's understanding of the Bible, are also priests are at the core of what an evangelical church of any denominational persuasion is all about.

In evangelical churches, the so-called laity are thus very much in the lead, and, in our case, the majority of staff are strictly speaking nonclerical in the denominational sense, including several of the most senior members of the leadership team, such as the leader (associate pastor) of the twenties and thirties group, HUB. While the "ordained" clergy do most of the preaching, lay members do sometimes preach as well. And often the person leading the worship service, including the prayers and communion, is part of the laity. (Regarding communion, evangelical Anglican parishes usually follow the same procedure as their Free Church colleagues—the communion elements come to you in your seat, rather than you having to queue up to receive it from a priest at the altar rail, as in Anglo-Catholic Anglican parishes and most Roman Catholic churches. Communion is seen more as a mutual sharing than as something you receive from a special caste of people in between you and God.)

Student Ministry

The largest single category of members of our staff work among students, as per our mission statement and in the light of Cambridge's particular university location. But perhaps the second biggest relates to our international ministry. The Bible shows Jesus telling his disciples to go out to evangelize all the different nations of the world—something we see starting in the book of Acts, especially after Pentecost. While our church does have a large number of people serving overseas as missionaries in the traditional way, we are fortunate in Cambridge that, in one sense, all the nations come to us!

At St. Edmund's there are normally between sixty-five to seventy different nationalities represented in the student body in any given academic year. The international inhabitants of Cambridge, however, are not found only among the university population (though that holds the largest number of them). As we saw earlier, thousands of language students attend English language courses in the city, and there are sometimes as many if not more of them than regular students at the colleges themselves, British undergraduates included.

With the opening of the European Union to Central and Eastern Europe, hundreds of thousands of immigrants from nations such as Poland have come to live in Britain, and a large portion of the Central/ Eastern European diaspora has come to the eastern part of England, with Cambridge being a magnet for many. Because of the recession in

Britain in 2008 onward, some of these new immigrants have returned to their home countries, but the population of non-English born Europeans is still very high. (For Roman Catholics, this has created a major logistical problem, since the number of Catholic practitioners is now the biggest in England since the Reformation nearly five centuries ago—many a Catholic parish has had a vast influx of Poles and Lithuanians and not enough priests to look after them.)

So our church, in collaboration with some specialist evangelical charities in Cambridge, has a much-increased international ministry. People coming from overseas often have considerable adjustment problems, and there are teams of Christians, many from our own church, ready and waiting at the Cambridge train station to help them make that transition from the moment they arrive. Among foreign students and academics at the university, there are large numbers of people from countries in which Christianity is forbidden or heavily restricted, and often such individuals want to find out about the Christian faith when they arrive, not least because they have the (sadly false) impression that Britain is a "Christian country." When they come to our church, they discover, as is the case of many evangelical churches in large cities as well as in university towns, that the congregation has people in it from all over the world, with Africans, Chinese, South Asians, Caribbeans, and others sitting alongside them in the pew. (We also have many interracial marriages in our congregation, a testimony to the global solidarity of evangelical Christianity.)

Church Planting

St. Andrew the Great also believes in church planting. This sharply distinguishes evangelical churches in the United Kingdom from similar churches in the United States and Korea, where the idea of a megachurch is quite normal: congregations of nine thousand or more are by no means uncommon in those nations.(Here I should say that I have the great pleasure of knowing the pastor and many staff members of one of the biggest and thriving megachurches in the United States, with whom, except on this issue of church size, I would be happy to claim much in common.) But in Britain, evangelicals see smaller local congregations as the best way forward in mission to their own country, as an integral part of the great commission, and, pastorally speaking, as a way of providing a place where everyone can actually get to know each other, something that is impossible in a church of nine thousand people or more, even if everyone can fit into one auditorium-sized service on a Sunday morning. This is part of the pain to which our mission statement refers. For us, nine hundred on a Sunday is a large number even when spread between three services (10:30 a.m. for families, 11:30 a.m. primarily for students, and 5 p.m. for the rest of us). So every few years we "plant" or "graft" a new congregation.

For Free Churches who can hire school halls for Sunday services, this is quite an easy thing to do. One of the most dynamic Baptist churches in Cambridge has done this successfully—the original mother church still meets in the formal setting of a Baptist chapel, whereas its daughter congregation, now an active church in its own right, meets each Sunday in a school hall, as do many of the other Free Churches in Cambridge, especially those of charismatic persuasion for whom not having a building of your own is almost a matter of principle (and a vast saving in maintenance and upkeep to boot).

Anglican churches have to work within the diocesan rules, however, so for us the process has not always been easy. Technically every part of England is a parish, so if you plant a new congregation somewhere, you are, by definition, intruding into someone else's parish territory. (Free Churches, being outside this constraint, can do whatever they like and as fast as they wish; as long as a friendly school rents you its gym, you are in business!)

Many evangelical Anglican churches do church plant, especially in London, where some, such as Holy Trinity Brompton and the equally revered St. Helen's Bishopsgate have done so successfully. St. Andrew the Great has planted three congregations, but our approach is different from some other Anglican churches. We find a parish needing support, a place where a large injection of new people will bring it back to life and growth again. So we essentially revitalize *existing* evangelical parish churches whose congregations might have dwindled, for a variety of reasons, by sending them around 150 members of our own current congregation along with one of our curates, who can then become vicar or priest in charge (the official term—not ours) of the renovated church. We did this first with a parish church in a village just outside Cambridge—which now has a church plant of its own—and then with two parishes within the city of Cambridge itself. (Our church plants tend to be more traditional than St. Andrew the Great, in that they do not have a large population of students and are usually more family-oriented, like typical churches elsewhere.)

This of course means that whereas most people stay with us, large numbers do leave, and the pain of separation is often a sad one, especially if, for instance, a home group splits up, with some of its members leaving and others staying behind. Financially too it is often very costly, since the donations of those setting off to the church plant are lost to us as they are transferred to help keep the new congregation going. It is to this as much as anything else that the words *pain* and *change* in the mission statement refer.

A church plant can therefore cause much pain in that, for example, half the youth group members can leave, all needing replacements, and the disruption this causes is by no means easy.

Pain can also mean accepting music you do not like. The amount of dissent in many churches over music—or *worship style* as it is sometimes called—can be epic! People of different ages—and evangelical churches usually do have a very wide age span—usually have dramatically diverging musical tastes, and, in any case, the music that we like often changes within ourselves as we grow older. It always impresses me to see congregants in their seventies and eighties accepting (or perhaps one should say *putting up with*) an incredibly loud volume of music of a kind that appeals to the student congregation at our 11:30 service (one member of our congregation uses ear plugs). But at a church that has as part of its mission statement the need to reach out to those of university age, most older congregants think it is a worthwhile sacrifice to have loud music. They would rather see hundreds of students flocking in each week, rather than be old-fashioned and traditional and thereby discourage those aged eighteen to twenty-one from ever coming through the door. Plus it should go without saying that the pain of worship music in the eardrum of someone over twenty-five is nothing compared to the far more serious and often profound pain that countless evangelicals suffer around the world.

Taking up Your Cross

But a proper evangelical, Christ-centered, biblical perspective is deeply uncomfortable to those living in our highly self-oriented, materialistic twenty-first century. The existence of change and pain is something that makes evangelical churches very different from many of the so-called *prosperity churches*, which, because of their congregational size and the popularity of their often flamboyant pastor, are alas all too frequently thought of as being similar or even identical to proper Bible-believing evangelical churches by the secular media. As our preachers often remind us, you cannot mention the cross of Jesus Christ too often! Christianity is and should be profoundly *uncomfortable,* since the gospel by definition challenges our natural self-centeredness and desire to go our own way.

A church, whatever its television profile or however gigantic its congregation, that packs people in by making them feel good about themselves is by biblical definition not Christian at all. It might have hymns, mention the Bible from time to time, and employ the word "Jesus" in some of its literature, but if one looks at the pattern of the New Testament, particularly Christ's frequent warnings to his disciples that if they follow him they will *inevitably* suffer, it should be abundantly clear to even the most secular of observers that such a church is a strange beast, and a million miles away from the authentic Christianity of the Scriptures.

Evangelicals, of all people, should be abundantly aware that those of us who live in the West have it very easy indeed. For as is obvious picking up a newspaper in the United Kingdom or watching the BBC, we see that *most* evangelicals around the world are suffering; just before writing this I received an e-mail about an evangelical Anglican Iraqi family being wiped out only days after the baptism of a member of their family, and that their deaths now make a total of ninety-three Iraqi evangelicals killed *in that one church alone in the past year*. Such very sobering statistics remind Western evangelicals that while we may be made fun of, or thought of as being quaint, or disliked by the secular politically correct, anything we go through is nothing compared to the intense suffering of our fellow evangelicals around the Two-thirds World.

Such deaths are not just things we see on the news—to us, they are *family,* brothers and sisters in Christ, in whose suffering we should share in solidarity.

No church is ever perfect! Nor should any church set itself up as a paragon of how best to do things. Evangelicals are, after all, the people who believe that all of us are by nature sinners, and that we are only saved by the grace and mercy of God. We should always look for the faults in ourselves and challenge ourselves accordingly; this is another key distinction, I think, from the kind of false churches where people go precisely to feel *good* and not be reminded of how bad we truly are! So in giving a description of my own church, I am of course aware that we are not perfect, as would (or should) all evangelical churches think of themselves. We are probably typical in our faults as well as our virtues, and there would doubtless be many criticisms outsiders could make about us of which we would be, alas, unaware.

Evangelism

St. Andrew the Great is also a church that wants outsiders to come in, as the mission statement makes clear. We engage in an enormous amount of quite unapologetic evangelism, preaching the Christian gospel and its uniqueness to all who come.

Our evangelism is, however, not just done through sermons, although there are special services from time to time, especially at Christmas, when people who do not normally go anywhere near a church feel quite happy to attend. Sermon-based evangelism on a Sunday is aimed at the regular congregation—students have university-based outreach, which our church fully supports, and our evangelism with students is designed to go alongside university-centered efforts.

We have, like many evangelical churches, adapted the *methods* of evangelism we use to the twenty-first century, while making it abundantly clear that the *message* we put across is the same as it was in the first century.

Because we minister in an increasingly postchurch age, in which fewer ordinary folk ever enter a church let alone listen to a thirty-minute sermon, we have our main evangelism outreach during the week, usually in our case on a Monday evening, and in a café-style format. (For a while we actually rented a real café, but now we recreate a café atmosphere within our own building.) About eighty non-Christians a week attend our Arena course, which explains the core beliefs of biblical

Christianity over eight weeks or longer. The setting is deliberately informal, but there is always a brief talk, and each week, every table at the café discusses a passage of the Bible. An experienced Christian is present to explain the message and to stimulate discussion among the non-Christian visitors, from whom any question is permissible.

If people do become Christians by the end of the course—and thankfully many do—they then join a second-stage course that explains their new-found faith in more detail, so they better know to what it is they have committed themselves.

Often people then join home groups and become integral members of the church itself, taking part in all the regular activities. Needless to say, those who have been converted through the course are often the best at recruiting others to come; their friends can see that their lives have changed and are often curious as to why!

We use the *Arena* syllabus. Much better known in Britain is the course founded by a large charismatic Anglican evangelical church in central London, the *Alpha Course* created by Holy Trinity Brompton.[1] *Alpha Course* uses a different format; it is carried out through dinner parties in the homes of church members, and it also has a strongly charismatic emphasis on issues such as the miraculous sign gifts, one that fellow evangelicals not happy with such a persuasion prefer to avoid. However it is fair to say that the basic principle is much the same—bringing the Christian message out to where people are and reaching those from an increasingly post-Christian background, whose busy lives often preclude coming to church in the same way as their grandparents might have done. One of the interesting facets of having Arena in a place such as Cambridge is the enormous number of non-British people who attend; as we saw earlier, the world is coming to Cambridge in a way unthinkable even a few decades ago.

What is interesting, too, is that it is the churches that unapologetically actually believe in something that are seeing new people come in, including a large number of scientists.

We are, as one would hope and as are most evangelical churches of any denomination or persuasion, *outward-oriented*. We do not exist just for our own members or to have a good time with like-minded people, although one hopes that church is a positive experience! We exist because we sincerely believe that what we teach is true, and that the Christian message is therefore the most important thing that anyone can hear and come to have faith in. For example, the terms *evangelical* and *evangelist* mean different things—a confusion common in the secular press. But both words are based on the word *evangel*, the good news of salvation centered upon Jesus Christ's life, death on the cross, and resurrection. So those who take the *evangel* seriously are bound to want to share it with others, and this is why evangelical churches are as they are—one trusts—in relation to *evangelism*, the sharing of that faith with others. And thankfully, in a church such as ours, it is plain to visitors that evangelical Christianity, and in an Anglican church at that, is most certainly no longer just the religion of white Westerners in a country of ancient Christian heritage.

The Picture of a Rural British Church

In addition to St. Andrew the Great, perhaps I should consider the practices of a small, picture-postcard, rural parish as well, since that is the kind of church that visiting Americans love to see and British people often regard (though not with any real historical degree of accuracy) as authentically English. I also chose this particular church for what it says about music, often the biggest source of controversy within churches and among outsiders when they look at, and misunderstand, what evangelical churches of any description are all about.

So let us take a typical small Church of England church—the kind of country parish that you see on television, not in the "God Slot" on British television, and certainly not the kind of megachurch that is televised in the United States, but the variety that you see if you watch a Miss Marple mystery, a rural church that is attended by much of the village and dates back perhaps centuries.

Churchill parish bears the same name as Britain's greatest prime minister, Sir Winston Churchill, and is not too far from where he is buried. This is what the church in Churchill, All Saints (and its neighbor parish, St. Andrew's Kingham), says about itself on its Web site (the Internet age has come even to ancient parish churches!):

There have been Christian churches in our villages for centuries, with St. Andrew's church in Kingham dating back over 900 years. Today the church here is very much alive as we seek to witness to Jesus Christ who is "the same yesterday, today and forever" (Hebrews 13 verse 8).

What are we like? We are an Evangelical Church of England church who meet in St. Andrew's, Kingham and All Saints', Churchill. As the word "Evangelical" is used in so many different ways, let us say what we mean by it! We mean that we believe that the Bible is the Word of God, written by men under the direct inspiration of God's Holy Spirit. Thus, as the Church of England's Thirty Nine Articles (written constitution) puts it, "Holy Scripture contains all things necessary for salvation." We therefore aim to build our personal and church lives on its authority.

We have a traditional communion from the Prayer Book every Sunday at 9 a.m. with a sermon but no hymns. . . . Our [main] service is from Common Worship (the latest prayer book). There we mix traditional organ hymns with more modern ones, either played through the sound system or, whenever possible, played by our own musicians. Our services centre around the Bible: it is read, explained and applied to the real world we live in. Bible readings and prayers are led by congregation members. There's loads to do and loads doing it!

We tend to think, don't we, that evangelical churches, or churches in general, are "out there" somewhere, certainly not what you would encounter in a thousand-year-old village church in the heart of rural England, and not that far from the quintessential and very English Cotswold countryside. But that is in fact just what we have here!

Look at what the church actually does: it mixes the traditional prayer book along with modern songs and a sound system. (A similar village community church, All Saints Little Shelford in the east of England, has a similar mix.) The secular press loves to refer to what it calls "happy clappy," yet often it has no idea that tradition and contemporary are not mutually exclusive, but frequently go together in churches that aim to be genuinely *inclusive*, with all varieties of worship patterns. But—and this is the key point—these churches focus on the importance of God's Word, the Bible, as being at the heart of all that they do, whether the music is centuries old in format or present-day and cutting edge.

In other words, what marks out an evangelical church are its core beliefs rather than any particular worship style. If my own church is anything to go by, many attending find, for example, modern worship songs far too loud, and their words lacking in the doctrinal depth and majesty of earlier generations' songs. But the sense of purpose in the service is always Christ-centered, God-honoring, and Bible-based, and this gives a focus to the congregation that unites them in common spiritual purpose more than the music styles divide them.

Capitol Hill Baptist Church's Vision Statement

Let us now look at an American vision statement, the 9 Marks of a Healthy Church, put together by Capitol Hill Baptist Church, a lively and flourishing congregation in Washington, DC. (The 9 Marks of a Healthy Church has been published as a book by the same name and is also online at www.9marks.org, where a great deal of additional material can be downloaded. Here I am giving my own take on the material, and would urge those interested to follow it up for themselves.[2])

Capitol Hill Baptist Church is one of the most dynamic of the Southern Baptist congregations in the United States. Its pastor, Mark Dever, is often asked to speak at conferences all over the United States. It is interesting (in the light of the politics chapter we will see later) that Dr. Dever is careful never to politicize his sermons, and he indeed has both Democrats and Republicans in his congregation, many of whom have connections with Congress, other branches of the government, and with the staff at the White House. But you will never get politics; his practice represents Mark 1, preaching not from the newspaper but from the Bible.

Although this is what a particular church in a major US city does, the 9 Marks are designed for all churches who want to follow this biblical pattern. And I would take it even further: this is a good indicator of what *real* evangelical churches are like not just in the United States, but also in the United Kingdom and throughout the world. In other words, Capitol Hill Baptist's approach to ministry is a paradigm of what any evangelical church ought to want to be doing anywhere, whether Britain or the United States, Nigeria, Guatemala, or South Korea. It is in that spirit that we now look at what Mark Dever and his congregation think are the nine hallmarks of a healthy, and, I would add, evangelical church.

1. Expository Preaching. In many congregations of a more traditional nature, the vicar or pastor uses what is called a *lectionary* (also used in Catholic churches), a list of prescribed verses that are to be preached upon on particular Sundays in the year. The verses need have no connection with what was preached last week, or for that matter any other week during the year. Often preachers will use something in the news upon which to provide a hook for the sermon, and so the congregation can attend having no idea what they are going to be hearing next!

This is not so in an evangelical church! *Expository* preaching means expounding the text of Scripture, often in considerable detail—working out what a passage in the Bible would have meant to the people who would have read it at the time it was written and what it is saying to us today.

Evangelical churches will work through whole Bible books. My church does this, as does Capitol Hill, often covering one book in the morning service and another in the evening. Some churches will take three months to go through a book, and then come back to it later; other pastors can take a whole year preaching through an Epistle, a Gospel, or an Old Testament narrative. But however long they take, evangelical preachers *always take an in-depth look at what that Bible book teaches*. This means that you are less likely to hear about the hobbyhorses of your preacher or something touchy-feely to give the congregation the warm-fuzzies, which is what sermons often end up being (all five minutes of them) in many other kinds of churches.

2. Biblical Theology. As the 9Marks people confess, theology is not usually a subject of the average Washington, DC, dinner party conversation! But it might well be among even the most political and dynamic of people attending Capitol Hill Baptist. (I have witnessed people on the White House staff discussing not inside presidential gossip but last night's sermon on Paul's epistle to the Romans.)

As we have noted, a hallmark of evangelicals is that they take the Bible seriously. They are the group that still believe in the great Reformation doctrine, *sola scriptura*; Scripture alone is *the* source of authority in what to believe and why.

Evangelicals have been called *bibliolaters*, or worshipers of a book, by those who do not give Scripture the place that we do. Such critics misunderstand why evangelicals give the Bible, and hence the theological system based upon it, such credence. It is not that evangelicals worship a book or treat the Bible in the same way that, for example, Muslims treat the Qur'an. It is God whom evangelicals worship, as, indeed, all Christians claim to do.

But how do we know what God is like? What is our source of knowledge about Jesus Christ? What is the main way of knowing what the earliest Christians taught and believed and how they behaved? The answers to all these questions are in the Bible. It is silly, evangelicals would argue, to say that you worship Jesus but reject the authenticity of what the Bible says he was like, how he lived, what he taught, and what he came to do. Scripture itself says the Bible is inspired by God the Holy Spirit, the third member of the Trinity.

Of course, there is still plenty of room for discussion about specific doctrinal issues! Capitol Hill, being Baptist, baptizes people one way, while, for example, Fourth Presbyterian, another well-known evangelical church in the Washington, DC, area, has a different theology and method of baptism altogether. But the key is that both churches hold to biblical theology, to working out what they believe on the basis of what Scripture teaches. The main thing is not that they disagree with each other on method, but that they agree with one another on *how to decide* doctrinal issues.

3. Biblical Understanding of the Good News. As 9Marks makes clear, evangelical churches *do not exist to meet the felt needs of their congregations.* This is important to remember, as many of the major churches in the United States and elsewhere (including even stiff-upper-lip Britain) do precisely this. These churches attract enormous congregations, especially among the affluent middle classes—Christianity-lite for yuppies so to speak—but alas also among the poor and needy, who attend in the hope that they too, like their pastor, will one day have a Cadillac of their own.

But this does not, or certainly should not, happen in evangelical churches, since the good news does just the opposite, making us all profoundly *uncomfortable*. As Jesus makes clear, time and again, humans are *all* sinners, in rebellion against God, putting ourselves and *our* needs first. What we *truly* need, to use the title of a book by Billy Graham, is not some kind of fuzzy good inner feeling, but *peace with God*.

This third hallmark is an interesting one, as it shows how bona fide evangelicals disagree with so many of the megachurches that you see on television whose pastors, often personally wealthy, have written the books that you see in many airport bookshops. (In fact, quite a few of the hallmarks that follow disagree with the bland megachurch way of doing things, not just in the United States, but in places such as Africa and Latin America, where similar megachurches exist.)

4. Biblical Understanding of Conversion. We do not go to church to make ourselves feel better, but to be restored in a right relationship with God the Father through the work of Jesus Christ on the cross at Calvary. In order to do this we need a genuine and *total* change of life and direction, one so profound that, as 9Marks makes clear, only God can bring about the transformation. We need the work of the Holy Spirit in our lives, convicting us of our own lack of righteousness, something the Bible makes evident we can never achieve for ourselves; we must instead accept what Jesus has done for us to make us right with God.

This is *conversion*, and, as we will see in chapter 4, evangelicals are very much conversion people: without it, you cannot be a Christian of any kind at all!

Back when Chuck Colson's famous book *Born Again* was published, writers on both sides of the Atlantic said that they did not like this *born-again* business, as if being born again made you some special kind of Christian.[3] In fact, they were right in one way to protest against the phrase "born-again Christian" because it is, if we follow what the Bible says about conversion, a redundant expression. There is, Scripture teaches and evangelicals believe, no such thing as a Christian who is not born again, for that is what a Christian is by definition: someone who *has* been born again! For if you are not born again, you *cannot be a Christian*.

Needless to say, this is not popular in many circles, and it is a belief for which evangelicals have been criticized for many centuries, but it is, nonetheless, the abundantly clear and explicit teaching of the New Testament. There is therefore, evangelicals would say, no option but to believe it. (It should become plainer, as the discussion progresses, why evangelicals hold to the view of Scripture being *normative*, to use a specialist phrase, in determining core belief. For if Scripture is not important, or if it's a matter of pick and mix, which is what many of the more theologically liberal persuasion would have us believe, then what a Christian is and how one becomes a believer could be based upon anything, or even nothing at all.)

The belief in conversion as being the only means of entry into the Christian faith also makes a huge difference as to how evangelicals preach to the unconverted, those non-Christians whom evangelicals would like to see come to belief and faith in Jesus Christ. Indeed, one could say that this biblical understanding of conversion is why evangelicals *evangelize at all*, since if there are many roads to God, then you could believe in the tooth fairy and still get to heaven, especially if you are nice to people around you and mean well. Evangelism, then, would not be necessary. But evangelicals strongly believe in sharing the good news.

5. Biblical Understanding of Evangelism. We must first take note that evangelicals still evangelize at all, which, in today's pluralistic age (when all faiths are considered equally valid), is a distinctly countercultural thing to do. In a postmodern world, no truth is absolute (except, as we saw earlier, *that* truth), and so the idea of evangelism, of persuading others that your truth is *the* truth, is to go against the very grains upon which our twenty-first-century Western postreligious society is based. With political correctness stating, for instance, that it is taboo for Christians to evangelize Jews or Muslims, and at a time when, in Britain at least, evangelicals are actually losing their jobs for so doing, one can see that this particular evangelical practice is far from popular! Yet this too has been a hallmark of evangelicalism since the Great Awakening of the eighteenth century (one of the biggest evangelistic outreaches of all time until the past few years), and, I would argue, a key doctrine of evangelicals since the Reformation itself.

Evangelicals are those for whom evangelism is at the heart of their faith and daily lives.

The *cost of conversion* is an old phrase that applies to millions of people today. Becoming a Christian can be a very personally costly experience, and can include losing a job, being ostracized by one's family, and in some countries, being sentenced to jail or even death.

You would not know this from some of the warm-and-fuzzy "evangelism" that you hear in some of the megachurches from the United States to Brazil. As Mark Dever and his team make evident, anything that says something along the lines of "just come to Jesus and all your problems will be solved" is not *biblical* evangelism at all. It might be splendid marketing—on the lines of "use this toothpaste and you will never have toothache again"—and it might even pack churches with the gullible, but it is not what the Bible has in mind at all.

First, evangelism needs to include the message of repentance. Second it much teach a lifetime commitment and leading a resolutely Christian lifestyle from then on! As the Dever commentary makes plain, there need to be *fruits* to prove that conversion is genuine, a revolutionary change of lifestyle and inner attitude. This will often involve huge sacrifice, even in countries where Christians are far from persecuted or even ridiculed. Sometimes being a Christian will involve not taking that pay raise, not taking a lucrative job, not going with the flow at work, abandoning a hedonistic lifestyle, and putting others, above all Jesus Christ, first.

Being a Christian therefore can be costly in terms of ambition, how others see you, what you can and cannot do ethically at work, how you spend your time and money, and what your life priorities and goals will be. If the evangelism is biblical, then it will be honest and mention all this, because when people become Christians, they will encounter, evangelicals believe, temptations and problems they never had before, precisely because they have become Christian. We will spend the rest of our lives fighting our natural instincts, which are, as the Bible shows, against God and spiritually worthless! Life becomes harder in many ways, not easier!

Again, this is not always popular. It is not the kind of message that gets you a TV show and books sold at airports. It is, however, what evangelicals believe that the Bible teaches.

6. Biblical Understanding of Church Membership. This hallmark may seem odd to some, especially those in traditional churches such as Church of England or Southern Baptist, for whom church membership is essentially a matter of geography and not of belief. But church membership is not a new topic for evangelicals, certainly not those in the United States and in other parts of the world as well.

Being a member of a church is not like being in a club. It is based upon whether someone is a true and committed Christian believer. So whether or not you can join an evangelical congregation has nothing to do with your niceness, bank account, winsomeness, good looks, family connections, brains, popularity, or any of the many other criteria that usually apply to whether you can join a particular club or society. The thing that matters is whether you are a member of *God's* church and thus want to become a member of a particular local congregation within it. And you cannot be a Christian by birth or by what country you were in when born. Being American or Welsh or of Puritan descent or of impeccable English breeding all make absolutely no difference to your being a Christian. It is the new birth *alone* that qualifies.

In the Bible, there are two kinds of church: the church universal, made up of all believers, alive or dead, from the beginning of time until the second coming of Jesus, and the particular local manifestation— what we read, for example, in Paul's epistle to *the saints in Ephesus*, those Christians living in that city at that point and time in history.

Evangelicals therefore believe that when you become a Christian, you are a member of the global church, and then must also be part of a local congregation, as was the case in Bible times. Evangelicals do not believe in freelance Christians, meandering around, not committed anywhere, and, as we shall see in Mark number 7, not under the *discipline* of an actual church.

This means that not anyone can get in! Many churches have discipleship groups or new members' groups to explain to new Christians what being a Christian is like in practice as well as in theory. Churches differ among themselves how they do this, but I think it fair to say that the net results are pretty much the same.

It is important to say that outside eminence makes no difference: One large evangelical church had the problem of someone *very* famous moving to the town and wanting to join that church right away. The Great Person was far too important to come to beginners' classes! (It is true that some churches highlight in their literature what famous people attend as part of marketing themselves as cool, or socially upper crust, or academically outstanding, etc.) The Great Person, in *worldly terms,* would have been a huge catch for this church and would have given it vast kudos in the competition with other churches in that town—*he* comes here, you know.

But the pastor refused! He told the Great Person that while he respected him enormously as a person and was honored to meet him, he could not change the rules of his church and allow the Great Person to jump the queue. Needless to say, the Great Person was not used to being treated like lesser mortals and went off in a huff, eventually joining another church.

Yet the pastor, for whom his insistence was no doubt costly, was being entirely biblical, and accurately following the Epistle of James, which makes plain that churches should *not* give undue or special place to outside criteria such as wealth or eminence. The English practice, in many an old rural parish church where the squire got a special seat to reflect his local eminence and social rank, is fascinating historically but also entirely unbiblical!

Nor should family get any preference either, as the third and fourth generation Puritans in New England America learned. As the Half-Way Covenant from the late seventeenth century shows, the leaders of Massachusetts and other Puritan-founded colonies had to wake up and realize that godly descent did not necessarily mean godly descendants. (We shall revisit this in the chapter on politics, when we examine the myth of "Christian America.")

So church membership is for believers only, for those who *really do believe.* In Baptist churches, often believer's baptism is given as an outward symbol of the spiritual change that has taken place in a person, but other denominations have different and, they would argue, equally valid means of welcoming people into the church family. But evangelical churches of all denominations usually have some kind of class, lasting several weeks long, to examine the depth of the faith of those wanting to join. These classes are especially important in churches where members have a vote and can therefore determine church policy, since you do not want people who do not *truly* agree with you deciding on what the church ought to do next.

7. Biblical Church Discipline. No one likes to be disciplined. But we know not just from family life but from schools, businesses, and many other walks of life that some kind of rule system and internal discipline is absolutely vital if society, or indeed anything else, is going to survive and to work properly.

So it is within the church. Discipline does not mean tyranny, as we see in all sorts of weird cults and some of the more extreme fringes of what pass for versions of Christianity. Even if the claims against Opus Dei are seriously exaggerated, no evangelicals ever have to whip themselves (as that group's members are purported to do), wear hair shirts, or perform some equally gruesome means of suppressing the flesh!

But church discipline is needed for a church to function both morally and doctrinally. Obviously there is a problem if the treasurer goes off with the funds or if the vicar goes off with the cleaning lady. But morals go further than that, despite outsiders' claims to the contrary, since the Bible makes clear that not only should Christians be moral in their personal lives but also, for example, in their professional working lives.

For Christians are part of God's plan for spreading the good news about Jesus Christ on earth. And non-Christians are right to be the first to complain if we preach one thing and practice another: hypocrisy is a major turnoff in any walk of life, from church to politics. If therefore we do *not* practice what we profess, we are not only harming ourselves but the message we proclaim as well, and that is sad news. It does no good to the gospel if a local Christian boss is widely and fairly regarded as a mean employer. Non-Christians will always know when we are being hypocrites, and the church to which we belong has the right to make sure that our lives are consistent with our professed faith—through discipline.

The same applies to doctrine, and this too is something to which the New Testament gives a considerable amount of space, not just in the teaching of Jesus in the Gospels but also in the Epistles, since even in the first century of Christianity people were already out to distort the message for their own ends.

Outsiders often criticize evangelicals for being too strict on doctrine! But these same outside critics would be rightly appalled if a group of which they were a member had folk within it who flagrantly taught something different from what that particular group or association had as founding principles. What would we think of someone who was an ostensibly keen environmentalist but had a gas-guzzling car and flew a private jet? We can all think of instances when people have professed one view and then led lives to the contrary.

A church needs to keep spiritual check on its members, to make sure that they really do understand the key doctrines. In many congregations this means that the members have the duty to keep an eye on the vicar or pastor! Many an evangelical church prefers its members to have their Bible open during the sermon so they can check for themselves whether the preacher is within biblical boundaries when expounding the passage, and sensible pastors always ask their congregations to keep them up to spiritual scratch. Discipline, therefore, in a proper evangelical church is as much bottom-up as top-down; there is no dictatorship here!

8. Promotion of Christian Discipleship and Growth. As the great twentieth-century evangelical Anglican pastor and writer John Stott once said, "Sermonettes breed Christianettes." We all prefer being adults to babies, and Christians are—or should be—no different in wanting to grow in their Christian faith as well.

That is why, for example, you will not find many five-minute homilies in an evangelical church. On the length of sermon, there is no agreement! But whether it is the twenty-five minutes of an evangelical Anglican church or the three-quarters of an hour to hour of many nonconformist churches in the United Kingdom and United States (and sometimes even longer in the Two-thirds World, where the whole service can last over two hours and more), the basic theme is the same. *Sermons matter.* Whatever your worship style, the basic theological point is that a sermon based upon the Bible is God's New Testament method of helping his people to grow corporately Sunday by Sunday. Evangelical churches across denominations and cultures hold to this. From London to Los Angeles to Lagos to Lima, sermons will be a key feature of any evangelical church.

In addition to Bible-based sermons, evangelicals emphasize discipleship. Churches differ among themselves how they do this—some in the United States have "Sunday school," where a more senior member of the church teaches and leads discussion on a passage or topic from the Bible. Others prefer, as we saw in chapter 1, to have small groups studying the Bible on a weekday evening. Either way, evangelicals take *individual* spiritual growth seriously. Since they are in the great Reformation tradition of the *priesthood of all believers,* individuals can read the Bible on a regular basis on their own at home, and they do not have to be led by one of the ordained members or staff.

Home groups, as we saw earlier, also provide mutual support. They help in terms of being able to help members talk through personal and spiritual dilemmas with fellow Christians in a small and secure setting. We can encourage one another with work problems, theological questions, and things in general that are on our mind.

There are, as is well known, many thoroughly evangelical megachurches, sometimes with over ten thousand people coming through the doors every Sunday. But evangelicals, as 9Marks makes abundantly clear on its Web site and in the accompanying book, are not *necessarily* devotees of the megachurch concept. While some of them do work very successfully and are much appreciated by the congregation, various things need to be noted.

First, many other evangelical churches, as we saw earlier in this chapter, are worried by the pastoral logistics of the megachurch concept. Having a famous congregation of ten thousand people sounds wonderful! But how on earth can you effectively pastor and mentor so vast a number of people? I know of one particular megachurch that breaks the congregation up into several Sunday schools, each of which has full-time people overseeing them, so that what you get is, in effect, lots of smaller churches meeting in the same building for separate Sunday schools and then all together for the main Sunday service. This can work very well. Many of the evangelical churches in the Two-thirds World follow a similar pattern, from West Africa to Latin America. Churches of vast congregations are by no means only an American phenomenon.

But both Capitol Hill Baptist and St. Andrew the Great do not follow this approach, and nor do many evangelical churches around the world. *Church planting*, as we saw, follows a very different pattern; when one church gets too big for everyone to know each other personally, ordinary members of the congregation as well as the leadership, a large body splits off and, depending on the original church's denomination, either forms a brand new congregation (the Free Church pattern) or grafts itself onto an already existing church that needs encouragement (the Anglican model).

But churches, if evangelical, that are bursting at the seams and those who deliberately keep themselves smaller have one thing in common: *quality is always better than quantity*. Size for the sake of size is as alien to an evangelical megachurch as it is to a smaller congregation. They all want to be churches in which many non-Christians are being truly converted and then grow spiritually as a result. Better to have five hundred Christians who are really going somewhere than five thousand pew fillers who are coming for entertainment and who see Sunday morning as an extension of their local golf club.

Numbers, evangelicals would agree, *can* sometimes mean that an extraordinary work of God is taking place. But it can equally mean that a flashy pastor is making thousands of yuppies feel good about their inner child, or whatever the fad of the day might happen to be. (An old acquaintance of mine, Professor Michael Horton, has written some wonderfully controversial books on this subject.[4] He may not be everyone's cup of tea, but if one is braced accordingly, his critique of so much of the lightweight froth that masquerades as twenty-first-century American "Christianity" is sobering reading [and proves to a non-US audience that Americans can and do know how to critique themselves.])

So size is not everything. Evangelicals see the need for converts to grow from drinking milk to eating real meat, and not stay endlessly at the baby stage (as the apostle Paul put it in his New Testament epistles).

9. Biblical Understanding of Leadership. The fish stinks from the head, and if the leadership of the church is going astray, there is every danger that the congregation will too. This is why the evangelical refusal to separate out clergy and laity is important, since the member in the pew has the right to keep a spiritual eye on the preacher.

But all the same, it is the leadership who set the tone, and, as we saw at the start of this chapter, they write up the vision statement that the congregation then approves and helps implement. Leaders and congregants alike are all under the authority of God's Word, the Bible. If the theology of the leadership is going astray, then spiritually speaking the church will itself be going nowhere, or in the wrong direction. For evangelicals, even to stay still is not an option—as the book of Revelation says in one of its nonperplexing chapters, the church at Laodicea was neither hot nor cold, but lukewarm!

We have looked in depth at an evangelical church in Cambridge, England; a small rural parish in the same country; and finally at not just the mission statement of one particular Southern Baptist church in Washington, DC, but a paradigm that is intended to be helpful to all evangelical churches.

As this book makes clear, evangelicals are to be found in all cultures and continents. Worship styles may vary. But the core truths and emphases remain the same, and the outward differences matter far less than the inward agreement. Let us go on therefore to look at how evangelicalism arose, and where it is going in the twenty-first century.

Three

Who Are Evangelicals?

For many readers who might not know any professing evangelical Christians, the answer to this chapter's question might seem a simple one, if what you see in the newspapers is any guide. An evangelical is a white, middle-class male Republican from the southern part of the United States (or, as we now have to add, a white *female* Republican from the rural West of America).

Now, for sure, many evangelicals would indeed fit into this description, and they are the demographic about which the mainstream news media writes the most. But, in truth, this description presents a highly misleading picture, and also a dangerous one, as it confuses evangelicalism as a whole, which is a worldwide, global movement, with just a tiny segment of it, and gives it a political coloring that is utterly atypical of evangelicals in most countries today. For it is now widely said that the average evangelical is an economically poor black Nigerian woman with numerous family members suffering from HIV/AIDS.

So wrong gender, wrong skin color, wrong country, wrong social class—in fact wrong everything when it comes to the stereotype of evangelicals we commonly see on television or in the newspapers. For the fact is that the overwhelming majority of evangelical Christians today do not live in the West at all but in what most commentators refer to as the *Global South,* or the Two-thirds World, since most of the world live there. These are often countries south of the equator whose level of economic development seldom matches the prosperity of the West, which experts define as the United States plus the western half of Europe. (China is usually lumped together with these nations, although when you look at a map, you will see that China is *north* of the equator, which puts that nation geographically more with Europe and the United States, which would not really be accurate in any other sense. But as hundreds of millions of Chinese still live in the kind of poverty we see in the Global South, and as a very large percentage of them are Christians, we can keep our generalization for now.)

Take the world's most international evangelical organization—the International Fellowship of Evangelical Students. As of 2008, this organization has over half a million members—students on the campuses of universities. Its chief executive is a French-speaking African from Chad, in West Africa. Its president is an Arab Christian from Egypt, and until recently its number two was a Jamaican. In many of the countries in which IFES works, Christianity is illegal, and so its work is clandestine. The key thing about it, though, is that it is run by the citizens of the countries themselves—Peruvians in Peru, Nigerians in Nigeria, Thais in Thailand, Hungarians in Hungary—and not by people from outside. This is one of the hallmarks of the global evangelical resurgence of the past few decades, and it has become one of the most controversial, since citizens of Global South countries often have far stronger attachments to certain doctrinal issues than their more accommodating (or perhaps simply fearful) fellow evangelicals in the West.[1]

There is, however, one thing about which the secular commentators are right: in terms of religious adherence, the United States in the twenty-first century resembles the rest of the world far more than it does the secular countries of Western Europe. In that sense, America is closer to Nigeria or Brazil than it is to France or my own country, Britain, both of which are highly secular, and, in the case of France, officially secular by law (what they call *laicity*). The exception would be the Northeast of the United States, once highly Christian and now much more akin to Western Europe than it is to the rest of the United States.

So what interesting things do we discover about evangelicalism when we look at the majority world, or Global South, or whatever we want to call it? One quick consideration first, and then our voyage can begin.

"The Next Christendom"

Here I am deeply indebted, as are all serious students of worldwide twenty-first-century religious trends, to the quartet of books by Professor Philip Jenkins of Penn State University in the United States.[2] His books are impressive, as he is a teacher at a *secular* American university and many of his works are published by Oxford University Press. He is clearly an outside observer making what he feels are objective judgments on the new global forms of Christianity—what his first bestseller calls "the next Christendom." Take some extraordinary statistics:

a. There are more Presbyterians in Korea, a nation that might soon be majority Christian, than there are in the United States.

b. The world's biggest Baptist church is also in Korea.

c. Half the people who attend church on a Sunday in London are of African ancestry.

d. There are between *seventeen and twenty times* as many practicing Episcopalians (or Anglicans) in Nigeria than in England, where the Church of England began. The vast majority of Nigerian Anglicans are evangelical, and Nigeria as a whole is 44 percent Christian.

e. There are more Chinese Christians than there are inhabitants of the United Kingdom—US government statistics say that there might be as many as *80 million Christians* in the People's Republic of China, if all the illegal, unregistered (and mainly evangelical) Protestant churches are counted.

f. Over 40 percent of Guatemalans and Chileans are evangelical.

g. Within the lifetimes of most of you reading this, countries such as Nigeria, Uganda, and Brazil will have far more Christians than the previous heartlands of Christianity in Europe and the United States.

In fact, the last point really only paints half the picture. As Jenkins points out, there are more church-attending Christians in Brazil alone than in the whole of the United States and Western Europe combined. Of these a rapidly growing number are not Catholics but Protestant evangelicals. Likewise, today around 40 percent of Ugandans are Anglicans—members of the worldwide Anglican Communion, of which the mother church in England itself is now a tiny minority—and the overwhelming number of Ugandan Anglicans are evangelicals. Not only that, but there are now reverse missions happening, with Anglican Ugandan evangelicals taking a lead in evangelizing post-Christian secular England. The former vicar of one of Britain's best-known evangelical Anglican parishes (Holy Trinity Brompton, the originator of the *Alpha* course), Sandy Millar, is now a suffragan (or assistant) bishop of a *Ugandan* diocese—a white Englishman subordinate to a black African on one level, but in a far more important sense, someone from a very secular country under the authority of somebody from one of the world's more strongly Christian countries, Uganda.

As we think of Africa, an important point needs to be made, one trusts without getting into too much political trouble. (We shall see later on that it is really only in the United States that one can draw a link between *political* and *religious* conservatism. In many countries there is no evangelical political default mode, and evangelicals are linked to all variety of ideologies, of the left, right, and more besides.)

One of the points that Jenkins makes, and I think entirely correctly, is that sociologists, including those whose main area of expertise is religion, tend overwhelmingly to be both inwardly secular and politically on the left. This, Jenkins argues cogently in several of his books, severely distorts how we see religion, and how we study phenomena such as the massive explosion of evangelical Christianity globally, outside the narrow prism of the post-Christian Enlightenment West, into which category most mainstream American universities would fall (even if the states in which they are situated are themselves religious).

Consequently sociologists tend to like looking at, for example, what they call the African Independent Churches (AIC). Unlike Jenkins, who is academically neutral, I hesitate to categorize such groups as "Christian," along with similar offshoots in the African diaspora in places such as Brazil. If these organizations and their millions of followers are counted among the "Christian" growth statistics, I might find myself sympathetic to mainline Catholics who feel that such groups should not really be counted, though I would of course disagree with them that there is no difference between such exotic creations and mainstream Protestants.

In addition, in many countries, "cradle Catholics," those who outwardly profess Catholic faith but who never attend a church, are, so far as experts such as Jenkins are concerned, counted in the statistics as Christian members of their country, such as in the United States. Likewise, most statisticians and commentators also agree that in England, while twenty-five million inhabitants firmly put themselves down as Church of England, only a million or so of those, a mere 4 percent, actually ever attend a church. To me, the main criteria is whether there is a link between *profession* and *practice*, something that does of course show my evangelical viewpoint, since to evangelicals, a Christian lifestyle is as important as mere words.

But in the Two-thirds World, at which we are looking, profession and practice do go very much hand in hand, since in these parts of the world Christianity is new; the nominal faith that we see in Anglicans in England and Catholics in the United States is still thoroughly foreign.

Nevertheless, to return to Africa, regardless of how one categorizes such AIC movements (such as the Kimbanguist churches, founded by Simon Kimbangu in the twentieth century), one statistic is vital: these AIC denominations *make up only 10 percent of professing Christians in the African subcontinent.* Sociologists like them because they give a fascinating and unique flavor, and they are, by definition, a breakaway from what such sociologists see as an authentically African rebellion against white Western forms of dominant Christianity.

However, as Jenkins also points out again correctly, all the undue attention the AIC receives is deeply resented by the 90 percent of African Christians whose profession of Christianity is entirely mainstream, and increasingly evangelical. They regard their own expression of Christianity as entirely authentic, and for white Western secular sociologists to deny their authenticity is to them insulting, if not racist. As Jenkins writes, by 2025 (now much closer than when he predicted this), there will be *400 million* professing Christians in sub-Saharan Africa alone. Even in terms of formal adherence to Christianity, sub-Saharan Africa, according to many observers, will already have displaced Europe as the chief Christian heartland within a mere quarter-century.

This change is one that will take a long time to percolate through to the consciousness of the secular media and academic worlds in the West—though one can thank both Penn State University in the United States and Oxford University Press on both sides of the Atlantic for giving somebody such as Philip Jenkins the opportunity to say things to both academia and the media that are abundantly obvious to the rest of us, but not to the denizens of the more blinkered audience that he is addressing.

Nonetheless it is now true: *African Christians are more typical of twenty-first-century Christianity*—and, I would add, *of evangelical Christians—than those in the now predominantly secular West.*

We are seeing evidence of this in some of the debates within the Anglican Communion. Historically, the Archbishop of Canterbury was seen *ex officio* as the leader of Anglicanism worldwide. This is now emphatically no longer the case, and not just because seventeen to twenty times as many Nigerians attend an Anglican church every Sunday than do Britains. Globally speaking, the focus both of numbers and of power has shifted overwhelmingly to the Global South, and this change has seen self-confessed woolly "bearded lefties" like Rowan Williams eclipsed by figures from Nigeria, Uganda, and other countries south of the equator. Archbishop Akinola of Nigeria speaks for a vibrant and growing church, Archbishop Williams of Canterbury for one that is in decline—except, that is, for its evangelical wing.

Secularization Theory

One branch of sociology has had a major problem with all of this. The growth of evangelical Christianity, and indeed of religion in general (such as the revival of Islam and Hinduism), has been a huge blow to those who held to what they called *secularization* theory.

According to this way of thinking, as we became more advanced technologically, medically, and in all sorts of other ways, religion, which these sociologists see as part of the premodern past, was bound to decline. Faith, to such experts, is no different from magic and other forms of ancient superstition, and however much we might enjoy the adventures of Harry Potter, we know that such things are just fairy tales with no place in the postreligious secular modern world.

However, apart from Western Europe, where one could argue that secularization theory did indeed come true—the religious are a rapidly diminishing proportion of the population in that part of the world—global statistics and evident experience show the exact opposite: now in the twenty-first century the world is becoming *more* religious rather than less.

Let us take another example of the rise of religion, courtesy of one of the other few sociologists of religion, Mark Juergensmeyer of the University of California, Santa Barbara, who predicted the rise not fall of religious adherence globally.[3]

In the 1950s the wave of the future in the Middle East was Arab socialism, embodied in the anticolonial figure, Gamal Nasser, the ruler of Egypt. Having routed the British and French at Suez in 1956, he was a hero of resistance against colonialism. But there is one thing that should be mentioned—while he was an Arab nationalist, the other ideology he possessed, *socialism*, is of course a thoroughly Western ideology. So while in one sense he was a secular nationalist against the West, in another he was totally Western in his ideological preference for socialism.

Consequently, when he and other local Arab leaders were trounced utterly by the Israelis in the 1967 war (a conflict that he had helped to provoke), the disillusionment among many Egyptians with the twin secular pillars of his regime, Arab nationalism and socialism, became very strong. Earlier in 1966, Nasser had ordered the execution of a very different kind of Egyptian ideologue, a Muslim scholar called Sayyid Qutb, who had been radicalized as a Muslim while living briefly in the United States as an exchange teacher. Qutb viewed Nasser as an apostate Muslim, someone who had betrayed the true path of Islam for Western views. But while Qutb was executed, his brother was not, ending up in Saudi Arabia where he taught a young idealist with a name we all now know well, Osama bin Laden.

The rest, as the saying goes, is history. Bin Laden's picture, now infamous, was on the front cover of Juergensmeyer's book about the rise of religious nationalism, *Terror in the Mind of God*, published presciently in 2000, some while ahead of the shattering events of 9/11.

According to the British journal *The New Scientist*, over 84 percent of the world today is religious in some form or another.[4] While this includes animists in the middle of rain forests and Western believers in the tooth fairy, it is, nonetheless, an astonishing statistic for the twenty-first century. If ever a theory has proved to be a complete flop, it is surely that of the inevitable rise of secularization. As we grow supposedly more sophisticated, we are getting *more* religious not less, though it is fair to say that we would have to include the extraordinary amount of superstition, of reading horoscopes and keeping crystals in the living room, along with a turning to the great historic religions, within the growth of religious belief. The great early-twentieth-century British thinker G. K. Chesterton expressed the idea that when people stop believing in God, they don't believe in nothing but frequently *anything*, and much of the modern world reflects that.

In particular, two kinds of religious faith are expanding at exponential rates, Protestant Christianity and Islam, in its different internal varieties (not just Shia and Sunni, but branches within the Sunni as well). German-based Arab writer Bassam Tibi has called this the *clash of universalisms*, and this too is further proof of how the secularists got it so wrong. (This is not the place to discuss Tibi's theories and other interesting debates, about which I have written elsewhere, as have many other commentators. Readers can find a large number of books on all this, especially post-9/11.) Christianity is a universal faith, in a way that an ethnic religion such as Hinduism is not, and Islam, while

Arabic in origin and language, makes similar claims to be a faith open to all races and nations.

Not only that, but it is *evangelical* Christianity that is expanding, and in parts of the world as diverse as Nigeria and Indonesia, often coming into conflict with a resurgent Islam. As the deeply Christian south in Nigeria expands northward, it meets up with an African Islam traveling southward, often with bloody results with Christians being put to death by angry Islamic mobs seeking to impose Muslim Sharia law upon the non-Islamic populations over which they wish to rule.

How is this?

I think that the answer, which both secular and religious writers now agree, is that the *absolute* nature of belief, both of evangelical Christians and activist Muslims, makes this kind of clash inevitable. So those who really do believe something are those who are growing, and those who prefer Western twenty-first-century postmodern angst are going nowhere, including those parts of Christianity for whom compromise with secular modernity is seen as the only way forward. There is indeed a wonderful irony in all this, because one of the main platforms of the liberal wing of Christianity is that only their de-supernatural brand will appeal to "modern people," yet globally it is precisely that watered-down version that is dying, whereas the supernatural-believing evangelical version is growing by leaps and bounds.

For while the supernatural may be regarded as somewhat weird in the faculty clubs of New England or in the dinner parties of the chattering classes in London, *it is precisely this feature* of evangelicalism that is giving evangelicals the cutting edge over more Western forms of theological liberalism. We just saw that most of the world is *still* religious, and while that may be unfashionable in some Western quarters, it is far different elsewhere.

Philip Jenkins mentions this phenomenon in his books, which has helped to make the case academically respectable, but countless missionaries on home furloughs from Atlanta to London will tell you exactly this, from personal experience. Let's look at demonic influence, for instance. Dealing with demons may not be something normal in many evangelical churches in Britain or the United States, although most would profess still to believe in the demonic at least in theory.

But in Africa, for example, the shadow of occult forces and the fear of spirit possession are still powerfully real—and, in fact, increasingly therefore in England as well, where thousands of the African diaspora now live.

Who wants watered-down faith when the local witch doctor has cursed your family? While writing this book, our home group in Cambridge, an academic city as we saw in the last chapter, just looked at the passage in Luke's Gospel in which Jesus cast out demons from a man traditionally called the Gadarene demoniac. For us this was a wonderful study of the power of Jesus over evil, and also proof that his power extended outside of mainly Jewish areas to those lived in by Gentiles. But if you live in West Africa, such possession is an ever-present real occurrence, and the fact that Jesus has power over demons and that Christians are protected by him and the Holy Spirit is a major advertisement for the evangelical version of the Christian faith. Much of the world still lives in fear of the occult, in Asia and in Latin America as much as in Africa, and the sheer joy and liberation from this debilitating terror is one of the greatest things that salvation in Jesus Christ can provide.

We know that the living conditions of many of the poorer parts of the Two-thirds World or Global South are not all that different from those in Old or New Testament times. But so too are the spiritual realities. This is unquestionably, the sociologists are now learning to agree, one of the most powerful reasons for the spread of evangelicalism in this part of the world. While white liberals want to think of themselves as progressive and as the most politically correct of all, it is again ironic that those in the Global South reject as Western and alien the form of spirituality-lite that Western *bien-pensant* liberals adopt. What sounds fine in Harvard or Cambridge is rejected as totally unrealistic and white in the parts of the world where the vast bulk of twenty-first century people now live.

Paradoxically, evangelicalism is so frowned upon in so-called "right-thinking" quarters of the Western intelligentsia because of this whiff of the primitive that people associate with it. Yet, and this is going to be our final irony in this chapter, that very view is of course profoundly racist! "Well they would believe *that* kind of thing over there in Africa. . . ." And yet many of these same people with these snobbish and condescending views were pillars in their youth of things such as the anti-apartheid movement and of trying to gain equal civil rights for those of different color in their own countries—all very commendable attitudes with which all decent evangelicals should agree. But when it comes to religion, the very continuation of which such people reject, it is a different story!

But one of the greatest things about true Christianity, and thus its evangelical version, is its egalitarianism. This too is one of its great sources of appeal in the Global South, since illiterate peasants have an equal place alongside Nobel Prize winners in the eyes of God.

These two things—the supernatural and the sense of equality—are of huge help in the struggle from Nigeria to Indonesia against Islam. For Islam too is a faith of absolute beliefs and of complete rejection of any kind of racial prejudice. The very absolute nature of evangelical belief, so off-putting to Western postmodernists, is its great strength when pitted against Islam, for Muslims too are firm believers in absolute truth.

One way Christianity has an advantage over Islam, sociologically speaking, is that faith in Jesus Christ empowers women in a way that Islam cannot match. All over Latin America, where Islam has not penetrated, evangelical women are liberated from machismo by the power of the gospel. When we look at the role of women in the New Testament, at how much women could and did do, we see a radically different picture from the inferior legal and social role of women in Islam. It is not surprising in the areas of the world where Islam and Christianity are meeting and clashing that millions of women are turning to salvation in Jesus Christ, who, unlike the chauvinists of his own day, would always speak to women, take them seriously, and use them in key roles in supporting the growth of the kingdom of God.

Evangelical Statistics around the Globe

Let us now look at some of the statistics that Philip Jenkins has used to get a more close-up picture of *global* evangelicalism today. Statistics are not usually interesting in themselves, but the ones that follow tell a fascinating story, so please persevere! (This data is from a mix of sources, including the *World Christian Encyclopedia*, which Philip Jenkins also utilizes, and from the *World Christian Handbook*, which is British-produced and not quite as up-to-date as the former.[5])

A couple of things to note: the *World Christian Encyclopedia*, regarded as the more authoritative in secular university circles, often splits evangelicals and Pentecostals. As we saw elsewhere in this book, I do not think that this is normally a legitimate thing to do. Certainly there are the wilder fringes of Pentecostalism that no evangelical would regard as being at all *evangelical* in belief, but here the important thing is that numerous Pentecostals would agree on the core evangelical basis of their faith. The encyclopedia also has a strange category of *Great Commission Christians,* which it separates from evangelicals in some cases but includes in others. I do not follow this: believing in Jesus Christ's Great Commission to go and reach all the world with the gospel is an integral part of the evangelical belief system, so to split groups up in this way is a mystery to me! Therefore I have interpreted some of the statistics in that otherwise essential and fascinating volume accordingly, and used the *Handbook* as well (though as we shall see, the *Handbook* was published some years earlier, and did in fact *underestimate* the growth of evangelicalism in some countries, whether deliberately or not, most notably in China).

Many African countries started to gain their independence around 1960, when Nigeria, for instance, became an independent nation in the British Commonwealth. That year, there were around 2.9 million people attending Anglican churches on the continent of Africa as a whole. By 1970 that jumped to 7.8 million, and by the time you read this it is expected to be about 24.6 million. That is an extraordinary statistic: an increase of over 800 percent in just a few decades. What is more remarkable is that in Anglophone Africa the Anglicans are the church of the former colonial masters! One would think that it would be the other way around: that as soon as independence came, the newly liberated peoples would cast off the yoke not just of political control, but of spiritual as well. Yet this was not the case at all—clearly far from it!

Likewise, the number of Catholics has risen in the same time frame from around 27 million to something approaching 115 million and more today, which is a quadrupling of the Catholic faithful in Africa, a continent where the overall population has almost but not quite quadrupled. So when the pope visited vast crowds of excited worshipers in Africa in 2009, , he was speaking to around 12 percent of the African continent in terms of ecclesiastical allegiance. (This is why, as we saw earlier, African Christians so dislike the Western sociologists spending so much time looking at the more exotic, and often doctrinally ambivalent, African Independent Churches. The vast majority, perhaps as much as 90 percent, of Christians in Africa are members of churches that we would recognize in the West, especially if one includes Pentecostal denominations. The churches in the latter group have increased about 2,000 percent, from around 1.7 million in 1960 to a projected 31 million in 2010.)

However one looks at it, all this is quite remarkable: Africa is becoming a *Christian* continent by leaps and bounds. And if anything, as we will see when we look at the projections from which Philip Jenkins quotes, the growth of African Christianity, evangelicalism included, is even more astonishing still, especially since in Africa (outside parts of southern Africa), "Anglican" normally means *evangelical* in a way that is not true in Britain and far from true in the United States.

The *World Christian Encyclopedia* provides extraordinary conversion figures for Africa. Some growth statistics inevitably include those born into church families. But in some countries we can actually see *conversion growth*, evangelical terminology that means becoming a born-again Christian, not because that is the faith of your parents or grandparents, but because you as *an individual* have come to recognize your need for repentance and *spiritual* new birth.

In Uganda, a nation Philip Jenkins has rightly highlighted, over 40 percent of Ugandans will be (if they are not already) professing *Anglican Christians*. These statistics include around *thirteen thousand converts a year* to the evangelical form of Anglican Christianity that prevails in Uganda. Denominations in the West of any description, let alone evangelical, would dearly love to have that kind of church growth!

In Nigeria, though, the numbers are even more dramatic. There the strongly evangelical Church of Nigeria, part of the Anglican Communion, sees around 167,000 converts each year join their churches.

That is almost the size of some entire countries in Europe or states in the United States! It is certainly bigger than the membership of some entire denominations in the West. This is spiritual growth on a most extraordinary scale, and shows that *globally* evangelical Christianity is on the rise, even while all kinds of Christian faith, evangelical included, are on the decline in the increasingly secular West.

According to the *World Christian Encyclopedia,* there will be around 34 million Anglicans in Nigeria by 2025, around a fifth of the entire population. In fact, the compilers estimate that by that year, 23 percent of Africans, some 136 million people, will be evangelicals, and of those there will be 76 million in the Anglican Communion alone. (This is using the encyclopedia's separate counting of evangelicals and Pentecostals; it reckons that of the latter, charismatics in mainstream denominations and Pentecostals in their own groupings will total some 227 million people. While some of the farther reaches of Pentecostalism would be beyond the evangelical pale, I think we could properly count most of that 227 million together with evangelicals, and say that by 2025 well over 300 million Africans will be evangelical Christians.)

In the United States, groups such as Presbyterians, which would include evangelicals in denominations such as the PCA, are holding their own but not increasing on anything like the same scale. The same is not true of Pentecostalism, however, which has had an eightfold increase, from just over 5 million in 1960 to an expected 40 million and more by 2010. If one considers that Pentecostals did not even exist in 1900, this is quite remarkable.

When it comes to Pentecostalism in Latin America we see an extraordinary story, going from just over 2.5 million in 1960 to just under 60 million projected some time in the near future. This is a twenty-four-fold rise or 2,400 percent, which is astonishing any way one thinks about it! The number of Pentecostal congregations similarly will have increased from just over 7 thousand in 1960 to nearly a quarter of a million within the next few years.

Even Baptists will see their numbers increase by around 800 percent, and Anglicans in the Southern Cone, the vast majority of whom are evangelicals, will soon have more than doubled. Latin America is well on the way to becoming as much Protestant in who actually turns up to church on a Sunday as Catholic—although the *notional* number of theoretical cradle Catholics will, of course, be far higher.

Likewise in Asia, Presbyterians will have quadrupled, to being nearly 17 million, and Pentecostals will have increased by over 1,000 percent in the same fifty-year time span of 1960 to around 2010.

In fact the one exception to all this astonishing growth is Europe, the most secular place on earth, with the Christian community of any description going down and not up, and with only Baptists and Pentecostals showing growth from the 1960s until now. (There are even several hundred thousand Pentecostals in Italy, a nation that one thinks of normally as being almost monolithically Catholic.)

Individual countries can also give an interesting picture. Take Guatemala, a country in Central America that has seen terrible violence and civil war in recent years, but from which it is now happily emerging. Here Pentecostalism is on the increase, so much so that Guatemala might even be a majority Protestant country in the not too distant future—it has already had presidents from the Protestant community, which can often be an indicator of future trends.

In 1960 there were not much more than 50,000 Pentecostals throughout Guatemala, but now there are comfortably over 2 million, an increase of something like 4,000 percent, or ten times the overall population increase of around 400 percent. Of Pentecostals (of which there are a bewildering number of denominations of which most of us have never heard), the Evangelical Assemblies of God is by far the biggest (of the Presbyterians in the country, which have decupled in size over a similar time frame, most are evangelical as well). In Guatemala's case, the old colonial power, Catholic Spain, left a long time ago, and the influence of the more Protestant United States has been deeper. That the country is now over 20 percent Pentecostal, not to mention the presence of other groups of Protestants, shows the wave of the future.

But it is interesting to note that although Mexico, which is right next door to the United States, has seen an increase in the numbers of Protestants, Pentecostals included, there are far fewer Protestants in Mexico, which has a total population of 115 million, than in Guatemala, which has around 15 million inhabitants, or just under a tenth of the population of its Central American neighbor. So whatever some Catholic sociologists might think, one cannot therefore associate the amazing growth of evangelical Protestantism in the region to proximity to the United States, since Mexico is not as affected but Guatemala is becoming more Protestant (and evangelical) by the day.

Chile is also an interesting country to study. If we add Pentecostals to evangelicals, some 40 percent of Chileans will be evangelical by 2025, in a country that is historically Catholic and where much of the Protestant missionary effort has for decades been that of Anglican evangelicals, with a major Anglican diocese based in Chile itself.

South Korea is also a nation in which Protestant Christianity is on the move. Here we consider the historic legacy of generations of American Presbyterian missionaries and the fact that the colonial power was Shinto Japan; Christianity in Korea was never associated with white rule—not that, as we see in Africa, that makes much difference.

So in Korea, while Pentecostals have risen, as elsewhere, from around 22,000 to just under 2 million, Presbyterians have risen from an altogether bigger initial base in 1960 of 1.2 million to well over 7 million today. This is not statistically as big a growth (700 percent compared to just under 1,000 percent), but for Asia, a Presbyterian community of such magnitude is unique, and again, a large preponderance of that 7 million is evangelical. In fact Korea sends missionaries all over the world, including secular Europe, with Korean Presbyterian churches being a global phenomenon. When we look over an even longer time frame, from 1900 to the present, we see that Protestants as a whole were 0.2 percent of the Korean population, then grew to something just under 19 percent today, or nearly 9 million altogether. If we add in the Korean Catholics, something like 40 percent of South Koreans are professing Christians today. Let us not forget: Korea was never under European rule, and yet it is on the way over the next few decades to becoming a majority Christian country.

In some countries the present-day statistics have by far exceeded the wildest dreams of those making the predictions in the mid-1990s. Around 1993 the Anglican Church in Nigeria was predicted to go from just over 400,000 at independence in 1960 to just under 8 million by 2010. In fact there are over 18 million Anglicans in Nigeria today, more than *double* the prediction. The Church of Nigeria, as it is technically called, has more people in church every Sunday than all the Southern Baptist congregations in the United States. We think, and with good cause, of the Southern Baptists as being one of the mightiest Protestant denominations in the world, one that has, in recent years, become predominantly (but not overwhelmingly) evangelical in its outlook. But the almost entirely evangelical Anglican Church in Nigeria is even bigger! I think few things can represent the astonishing growth of evangelical Christianity in the Two-thirds World than that: there are more Nigerian Anglicans than American Southern Baptists! As I have said elsewhere in this book, when we think of a typical evangelical, we should picture a black financially poor Nigerian Anglican from Africa, rather than a stereotypical white middle-class Texan Southern Baptist! In fact, some statisticians say that if the Nigerian Anglican Church were a denomination in its own right, it would be the fourth biggest in the world.

But all this still pales into insignificance when we consider the probable rise to just under *100 million* Christians currently in China. Here statistics differ wildly. The CIA and United States Commission on International Religious Freedom figures indicate at least *80 million*. The *World Christian Encyclopedia* (which underestimated the projected number of Nigerian evangelical Anglicans by several million) reckons that of just Protestant Christians, the government-sponsored Three-Self Patriotic Movement will soon have around 9 million adherents, and the so-called *house churches*, those that meet clandestinely without government approval or license, will shortly have over 85 million. Combine those two to get 94 million, and then add in the numbers of Catholics (again in two groups, one approved by Rome and the other approved by Beijing), and one reaches comfortably *over 100 million* Chinese citizens, in a Communist country, attending church every Sunday.

Statistics are notorious for being potentially unreliable, both here and in general, and especially as the bulk of these Chinese Christians are in churches unrecognized by the Chinese government, and who might therefore not wish to be openly counted in official statistics. The Three-Self Patriotic Movement has what seems to be around one-ninth of the overall attendance of the underground house churches. It is also possible that there might be some double counting, with some Christians attending both kinds of church, tolerated and illegal. And obviously, by definition, if a church is clandestine, getting precise figures is going to be hard! So the American figure of around 80 million plus might be safer on which to rely. But either way, 80 to 100 million is still a lot of people, especially for an Asian country that is still Communist, and therefore atheist in its outlook.

While I was studying for this book, the London *Times* fortuitously published an article in March 2009 that showed that these statistics are recognized by secular statisticians as well as Christian—they put the number of Christians in China in 2009 at well over 100 million. What is even more astonishing is that 74 million Chinese are members of the Communist Party; for many, their membership is almost certainly more pragmatic—necessary to get a good job or make business connections—rather than ideological. There are, whatever way you look at it, millions more Christians in China than members of the Communist Party. As the article made clear, Protestant Christians, both official Three-Self and unofficial unregistered, are usually evangelical in tone (this is a theological distinction one does not normally expect in a secular British newspaper), so that, I would add, one can say that there are more *evangelicals* in China than Communists.

Considering that the atheist Communist Chinese expelled all missionaries in 1951, and then between 1966 and 1976 tried to eradicate religion of all kinds from China—Buddhist, Daoist, and Confucian as well as Christian—that statistic is quite mind blowing! As the *Times* wrote, some 10 percent of the Chinese population, the largest on earth, are now Christian. How the nineteenth-century missionaries from Britain and the United States would be amazed!

When one considers what the Bible calls the "cost of discipleship," the persecution that Christians often face because of their faith, the enormous cost in many regions of China is quite appalling even today. In China, professing Christian faith is not something done lightly. And the majority of those in the unofficial churches, as reported by those who visit with them regularly from the outside and are in a position to know these things, are what we in the West would consider as being evangelical in theology.

So the country with the world's greatest number of evangelicals in the twenty-first century could indeed be the People's Republic of China! Could those brave missionaries from Britain and the United States in the nineteenth century ever have thought it? Going to China was not the "white man's grave" (a few years of service followed by an early death) that a missionary in West Africa often faced—but with transport in the Victorian era not being what it is now, leaving the West for China was often a lifetime commitment. Now, in the twenty-first century, overt missionaries are illegal, but the evangelical and all other kinds of Christian population of China probably exceeds the *total* population of even the biggest countries of Western Europe, such as Germany, France, or Britain. Such has been the changing nature of Christianity in the twentieth and now twenty-first centuries.

Four

Evangelicals Past and Present

Historically speaking, evangelicalism is supposed to have begun with the Great Awakening in the eighteenth century, a transatlantic phenomenon. Similar evangelical movements have also reflected both a British and an American dimension, such as a major turning to Christian faith, called a *revival* (in the British sense of that term) in 1859. In particular the United States saw great evangelistic activity and a turning to Christian faith on a large scale associated with the ministry of Jonathan Edwards, and Britain saw similar revival with the brothers John and Charles Wesley. George Whitefield figured prominently on both sides of the Atlantic.

Four Characteristics of Evangelicalism

Historians such as David Bebbington in Scotland have noted four main characteristics of the growth of evangelicalism at that time.[1] These are:

1. *Conversionism*: the belief that lives need to be changed
2. *Activism*: the expression of the gospel in effort
3. *Biblicism*: a particular regard for the Bible
4. *Crucicentrism*: a stress on the sacrifice of Christ on the cross

As Bebbington reminds us, leaders such as John Wesley, one of the founders of Methodism, emphasized the first two: conversion, being "born again," or what theologians call "justification by faith"; and the necessity of being saved through accepting Jesus Christ as Savior through Jesus' sacrificial death on the cross, what theologians call the *atonement*.

With all this, evangelicals are in full agreement today, in the twenty-first century.

Here I should note that these four points are certainly what evangelicals *ought* to believe as their foundational doctrines, as we saw in the IFES basis of faith in chapter 1. However, as younger scholars such as Michael Horton and older preachers such as John MacArthur have pointed out, often in controversial books, there is sometimes quite a difference between *theoretical belief* and *what evangelicals do in practice*.

This is not the place to argue these much debated points! Suffice it to say that some authors and preachers—notably the two in the last paragraph—have pointed out what they feel is a major cultural compromise by many (but not all) evangelicals, in going along with the touchy-feely, faith-meets-my-felt needs, me-centered culture of the late twentieth and early twenty-first centuries. And it is certainly true that those who do preach what one might call *Christianity-lite* have packed congregations, hosted television shows, and written bestselling books you find at airport bookstores.

However, while I have the pleasure of knowing these two people, in this chapter I am going to accentuate the positive and concentrate on historic evangelicalism (to which they too also fully adhere). I will leave any negative commentary on the various weird and wonderful postmodern strains of what they and I would agree on as being pseudo-Christianity to other heavyweight commentators and theologians who have examined such trends in depth. What you are getting here is the original, historic evangelicalism, which is the same in the United States and the United Kingdom and which is becoming the norm in most of the developing world (where it is, in effect, *the* predominant version not just of evangelicalism but of Christianity itself).

We could say a great deal about the "Bebbington thesis" of evangelicalism, especially regarding these four crucial characteristics, which arose from the Great Awakening and have been a vital part of Protestant Christianity down to our own times. However, I do sympathize with what John Stott, one of the three or four most internationally influential twentieth-century evangelicals, has said, namely that *evangelicalism is simply mainstream Christianity.*[2]

In other words, while from a *historic* viewpoint (and your author is also an historian) the present manifestation of evangelicalism might indeed have some of its roots planted in the extraordinary spiritual growth of eighteenth-century America and Britain, *theologically* evangelical faith goes right back to the beginning of the church itself, a theme I have followed elsewhere, in *Church History: A Crash Course for the Curious.*[3] Evangelicalism in this sense is not new at all: it was what the Christians at the time of the Bible thought, what the early church taught, and what the reformers of the sixteenth-century also believed.

There has therefore been a strong continuity throughout history, and what we see in the eighteenth century is not at all a new phenomenon, but perhaps a re-expression of old truths conveyed in new ways that reached a different audience. This is like, if you will, an English Standard Version to update the King James Authorized Version. The message is identical, but the language in which it is expressed is new. (This is of course a Protestant point of view. Catholics reading this will not agree, since they see a direct continuity from the early church right through to the present day fulfilled only in the doctrines and practices of the Roman Catholic Church.)

It was on precisely these characteristics that the Reformation was fought. *Sola fide,* by faith alone, is 1 and 4 above, just as Wesley suggested, and 3 is *sola scriptura,* Scripture alone, a Protestant way of saying that only the Bible determines what Christians believe, and not the authority of church tradition (the Catholic view).

Activism

What is new, perhaps, is 2, *activism*. This is not a new *doctrine* but an additional emphasis; if the other three things are true, then it is the duty of true Christians to get involved in the society around them and to try to change it in a godly way for the better. From the time of the Great Awakening to the late-nineteenth/early-twentieth centuries, evangelicals were at the forefront of social change and improvement (until what historians call the Great Reversal, when evangelicals tragically, I would argue, stopped being what the Bible calls "salt and light" in society and retreated into a hidey-hole, emerging only to evangelize but no longer to transform the world in which God put them).

During the Reformation, Protestants still saw everything as being done through the state, which became Protestant instead of Catholic. (There were exceptions such as the Anabaptists—today's Mennonites— but at that time they were very much the exception.) By the eighteenth century the state might still have been Protestant, but *spiritually* speaking it was no longer, if it ever truly had been, sympathetic to the doctrines that believing Christians knew to be vitally important. Evangelicals therefore had to mobilize supporters for what they saw to be the key issues of the day, since the state would not do this for them. In the late eighteenth century in Britain and well into the nineteenth century in the United States, *the* issue about which evangelicals became activists (to use the Bebbington term) was slavery.

The two hundredth anniversary of the historic abolition of the slave trade in the British Empire was celebrated in 2007 (1807–2007; slavery itself was not abolished in British realms until the 1830s). Thanks to the film *Amazing Grace* we are now all familiar with the great British hero of the abolition movement, William Wilberforce (1759–1833).[4]

Wilberforce is a classic example of evangelical activism in the best sense, of seeing the duty to love your neighbor as yourself as something necessary to do alongside preaching conversion to those who do not know the message of salvation on the cross. He was a politician, but one who never held high office, since he devoted his political career to the great movement to end the slave trade and then to abolish slavery itself.

It is important to remember that Wilberforce believed in both sides of the evangelical life—Christian mission and Christian social action— and did not see the two as incompatible. He was as much a writer of serious Christian literature as he was an abolitionist. He was actively involved in Christian mission to Africa in terms of winning converts as well as a person who wished that people from Africa were no longer enslaved.

He was also careful to be supported by a coalition of fellow evangelical activists, who were given the nickname of the "Clapham Sect," named for the part of London in which many of them lived. Among these was a lady who one might describe as one of the earliest public policy intellectuals, Hannah More, a woman who showed that, like Selina Countess of Huntingdon in the eighteenth century, women could be as actively involved in major campaigns as men.

We know that Wilberforce's campaigns ended happily, and that in Britain, alas as opposed to the United States, slavery was abolished without great conflict. But it was a lifetime's campaign, decades long (something that the film does not portray adequately), and took an enormous amount of personal faith and persistence by Wilberforce and his supporters. They acted as they did *because* they were evangelicals, because they knew that slavery was morally wrong and that it was incompatible with what they understood to be the clear teaching of Scripture on the subject.

But they also were careful to be sure that their arguments would appeal to others, because evangelicals, the Great Awakening notwithstanding, were a small minority in Britain even then. They also did not attempt to link their campaigns with *party* politics. Wilberforce was a Tory (the forerunner of today's Conservatives), but that did not mean he ostracized the Whigs, the rival party (ancestor's of today's Liberal Democrats), because abolishing slavery was a cause for which they wanted to win over as many people as possible.

The same is true of another major British reformer of the nineteenth-century era of evangelical reform and philanthropy, Anthony Ashley-Cooper, seventh Earl of Shaftesbury (1801–1885). He was a hereditary politician as a member of the House of Lords, and someone who, like Wilberforce, never held high government office, despite, in his case, being related by marriage to the Whig Prime Minister, Lord Palmerston. Shaftesbury's great concern was the appalling way in which children, often extremely young, were forced into working in mines and factories, none of which had any of the safety features that we take for granted in the workplace today. He was responsible for two Factory Acts in the 1840s that explicitly forbade child labor and a Mines Act that had a similar effect.

But Shaftesbury was not just a reforming politician. He was president of the Evangelical Alliance and also involved with many mission agencies, including one that lobbied for the physical return of Jews to Palestine long before that became politically possible in the twentieth century.

Shaftesbury, like Wilberforce, did not see any discrepancy between being involved *as an evangelical* in social activism while at the same time promoting evangelism and conversion through Christian mission. As he famously put it, the God that made people's souls made their bodies as well, and there is thus no divergence between wanting them to become Christians but also caring for them physically as human beings made in God's image. Shaftesbury also was careful not to make his campaigns party political, since he too needed support from all sides.

There were plenty of other major reformers in the nineteenth century who were passionately evangelical and active in the public sphere in terms of trying to improve the world in which God placed them. One of these was a woman, Elizabeth Fry (1780–1845), who was instrumental in achieving major prison reform (British prisons had been barbaric places). Fry was successful despite the fact that women did not have the vote until 1918, decades after her death. Like her was Thomas Barnardo (1845–1905; known simply as Dr. Barnardo, as he was a medical practitioner), whose homes for orphans and similarly disadvantaged children were a massive improvement over the soulless and often brutal local orphanages of his day. (His work among orphans still exists today, as do, in a different form, the Spurgeon's Homes, the refuges for children set up by the great Baptist preacher, Charles Haddon Spurgeon, at around the same time.)

However, both Britain and the United States then came to the Great Reversal, the decision by evangelicals on both sides of the Atlantic to opt out of public life and to concentrate on evangelism only. Bebbington wrote:

The gospel and humanitarianism . . . were not seen as rivals but as complimentary . . . Although the career of [Lord] Shaftesbury was never forgotten, it is remarkable that the charitable theory and practice of the mass of nineteenth-century Evangelicals were to be minimised by later commentators. Probably the chief explanation is that Evangelicals of the nineteenth century have been tainted by the repudiation of Christian social obligation that marked certain of their successors in the following century. In the nineteenth century, however, even if private philanthropy was common in all religious bodies and beyond, Evangelicals led the way. Among charitable organisations of the second half of the century, for instance, it has been estimated that three-quarters were Evangelical in character and control.[5]

That last figure is in itself astonishing, and shows the enormous *societal* impact that an evangelistically active and socially aware evangelicalism had upon its own society. For instance, the Salvation Army in Britain has strongly evangelical roots, whatever individual members might be like today, and that organization explicitly connected evangelism with social concern.

Unfortunately, in late nineteenth-century America (and to a less-marked extent, Britain as well), preachers such as the famous evangelist Dwight L. Moody began to preach that *only* conversion mattered. He also placed far more emphasis on the *individual* and on the need for *personal* repentance—all important historic evangelical concerns and emphases—and away from the idea of evangelical *corporate* action to transform society.

So unfortunately a dichotomy arose—*either* evangelism *or* social concern, but not, alas, *both*. As a result those of liberal theology, for whom the biblical emphasis on the new birth and being born again was alien or ignored, were able to reach in to fill the vacuum that evangelicals had created. Soon the Social Gospel—what we might describe as Christianity-lite, with all the foundational spiritual and theological components stripped out—took over. Social action, instead of being a natural corollary of an evangelical Christian worldview, became a watered-down substitute for the original by people whose attachment to the specifically spiritual side of Christianity was somewhat tenuous.

Thus by the 1920s evangelicals regarded social activism—so familiar to their nineteenth century evangelical precursors—as now the exclusive preserve of theological liberals, and thus something to be spurned at all costs.

Today this divergence is slowly being overcome, with evangelicals once again becoming involved in societal issues, and not just those of personal morality, such as abortion. Evangelicals are also becoming involved in environmental concerns, for instance, with leading 1970s evangelical and thinker Francis Schaeffer, an American living mainly in Switzerland, blazing a trail. His rare book gave a specifically evangelical theology of the environment long before others even recognized it as an important issue, let alone one about which evangelicals should concern themselves.

In Britain, thankfully, evangelicals are not automatically associated with any particular political party; there are evangelicals in the Conservative, Labor, Liberal Democrat, and other political parties. And so, as in the nineteenth century, evangelical social action is taken seriously by secular politicians of all stripes. For all sorts of historic and cultural reasons, many specific to the United States, this is not quite the same on the other side of the Atlantic, where evangelicalism is still closely associated with the Republican Party, notably on the issue of abortion. Worldwide, however, the situation is much more similar to Britain, and evangelicals can get involved in issues of social and economic justice—and of personal morality—without being associated in the public mind as inevitable followers of a particular political party.

Perhaps the Great Reversal is being reversed and all four of the evangelical distinctives of the Great Awakening of the eighteenth century are coming back.

Conversionism

Conversionism is as active as it ever was. We saw earlier that evangelicals have historically collaborated across denominational divides, and regarding the specific issue of evangelism, of going out and winning converts, evangelicals have been as busy as ever in their history.

One of the major evangelists of the twentieth century *not* to mire himself in controversy or scandal is Billy Graham, someone who merited a major profile in *Time* magazine as recently as 2007, despite the fact that now, due to ill health, he is no longer able to lead missions in the way that he once was.[6]

Graham's Crusades were always, by definition, multidenominational and unashamedly evangelistic. (In fact he would have people on his platform who were not evangelical, which led him to be treated warily by fellow evangelicals for whom this was going a step too far.) He was also careful to work with local churches, so that bringing friends to a Billy Graham Crusade was, properly speaking, the result of much *local* effort, of ordinary Christians using his presence in the area to bring their non-Christian neighbors to hear the famous preacher.

Today there are not many people, if any at all, who have quite the international fame of a Billy Graham. In the West, and particularly in the United States, some tend to politicize him, to associate him with the infamous Richard Nixon, who was ruthless in the way in which he would manipulate his connections with the frequently politically naïve Graham. When I wrote about Graham in the mid-1980s, his close friends, the Wilson brothers, looked back on that whole episode with embarrassment, on how they were snared.[7] Graham himself told me (in 1983) that in terms of his own efforts in the 1950s to bring about racial reconciliation in the American South—in which he played a positive and wholly pivotal role—the president to whom he was the closest was Lyndon Johnson, a Democrat.

But regardless of his political associations, Graham was one of the first leading Western Christians to spot that the center of gravity in Christianity was shifting from the West, including the seemingly all-powerful United States, to the Global South, to the Two-thirds World. So while in the United States he is often remembered for unwise political friendships as well as for his Crusades, and in Britain for transforming the nature of evangelism by his gigantic Crusade in London in 1954, in many other parts of the world he is revered for being the person who had the international reputation and authority to recognize that the days of Western leadership of Christianity were coming to an end.

Some of Graham's Crusades were in places such as India. There he was always keen to be culturally sensitive, and only to do things in a way that the local Indian Christians found acceptable; he did not want to make the mistake of leading others to equate Christianity with the West.

But more important, he realized that the key to Christian growth in these countries would not be Westerners like himself parachuting in from the outside, but *local* evangelists reaching out to their own people, in their own language—not on the scale of a Graham Crusade, but faithfully, slowly but surely, over many decades. In this he was changing the method of Western missionary activity from the past and allowing local Christians to run things their own way in their own countries.

The fact—for that is what it is—that Christianity is centered in the Global South is something that is only now dawning upon the consciousness of the academic and media worlds in the West, thanks to academics such as Philip Jenkins. But this is something evangelicals have realized for a while, since leaders such as Martyn Lloyd-Jones (and the creation of IFES) in the 1940s and Billy Graham and John Stott in the 1960s and 1970s.

Graham had a major training conference in Berlin in the 1960s. But the gathering that recognized the historic transformation of global evangelicalism, and indeed of all forms of Christian faith, was the Lausanne International Congress on World Evangelism in 1974, held in the Swiss town of that name. At that gathering, both Graham and Stott, who was acting as a kind of drafter-in-chief for all the various resolutions, effectively allowed their fellow evangelicals of the Global South to take over the proceedings and to determine the agenda. No longer could evangelicalism be said to be led by white Westerners, but now by Latin Americans, Asians, and Africans. It became a *partnership*, between Christians in the West and the majority in the Global South.

The Lausanne Covenant

When I had to choose a basis of faith as a classic example of what evangelicals believe, I chose that of IFES, as it is a movement within global evangelicalism with which I have been closely linked for over thirty-five years (and my family for over sixty). Nevertheless, I think it is also worth looking at the Lausanne Movement's covenantal statement, not in great detail, as we did with that of IFES and my church in Cambridge, but to show how evangelicals have come from being a Western phenomenon to being the global movement that they are today.[8]

The Lausanne Covenant was hammered together in 1974 by evangelicals from West and South, and all under the benevolent eye and encouragement of America's most famous evangelist, Billy Graham. It is *this*, I would argue, that is the true Graham legacy.

This statement is often radical, and with the degree of emphasis it places on spiritual warfare, it perhaps goes further than many might be happy with in the West. But Jenkins has pointed out in his many books, it is precisely *this* that wins so many in the Two-thirds World to evangelical Christianity, since in many parts of the globe the feeling of the spirit world's real presence has never gone away. It is the liberal denominations, with their post-Enlightenment rejection of the supernatural, who are losing out, and it is the evangelicals, who recognize that there is a major spiritual battle (however one wants to express it), that are winning the hearts and minds of those in the Global South.

Note what the covenant says about issues such as culture and persecution. No longer is Christianity something brought by white people in a safari helmet! The old nineteenth-century identification of Bible and flag has gone. Note too that it affirms that Christians are sure to be persecuted—something that is as much a reality in the twenty-first century as it was for the believers in the early church. Note also that it has no problem linking together evangelism and social action, and that it was Billy Graham, so often linked with Nixon, who was signing off on such a statement in 1974, the year of Nixon's resignation after Watergate.

___

Introduction

We, members of the Church of Jesus Christ, from more than 150 nations, participants in the International Congress on World Evangelization at Lausanne, praise God for his great salvation and rejoice in the fellowship he has given us with himself and with each other. We are deeply stirred by what God is doing in our day, moved to penitence by our failures, and challenged by the unfinished task of evangelization. We believe the Gospel is God's good news for the whole world, and we are determined by his grace to obey Christ's commission to proclaim it to all mankind and to make disciples of every nation. We desire, therefore, to affirm our faith and our resolve, and to make public our covenant.

1. The Purpose of God

We affirm our belief in the one eternal God, Creator and Lord of the world, Father, Son, and Holy Spirit, who governs all things according to the purpose of his will. He has been calling out from the world a people for himself, and sending his people back into the world to be his servants and his witnesses, for the extension of his kingdom, the building up of Christ's body, and the glory of his name. We confess with shame that we have often denied our calling and failed in our mission, by becoming conformed to the world or by withdrawing from it. Yet we rejoice that even when borne by earthen vessels the gospel is still a precious treasure. To the task of making that treasure known in the power of the Holy Spirit we desire to dedicate ourselves anew. (Isa. 40:28; Matt. 28:19; Eph. 1:11; Acts 15:14; John 17:6, 18; Eph. 4:12; 1 Cor. 5:10; Rom. 12:2; 2 Cor. 4:7)

2. The Authority and Power of the Bible

We affirm the divine inspiration, truthfulness, and authority of both Old and New Testament Scriptures in their entirety as the only written word of God, without error in all that it affirms, and the only infallible rule of faith and practice. We also affirm the power of God's word to accomplish his purpose of salvation. The message of the Bible is addressed to all men and women. For God's revelation in Christ and in Scripture is unchangeable. Through it the Holy Spirit still speaks today. He illumines the minds of God's people in every culture to perceive its truth freshly through their own eyes and thus discloses to the whole Church ever more of the many-colored wisdom of God. (2 Tim. 3:16; 2 Pet. 1:21; John 10:35; Isa. 55:11; 1 Cor. 1:21; Rom. 1:16, Matt. 5:17, 18; Jude 3; Eph. 1:17, 18; 3:10, 18)

3. The Uniqueness and Universality of Christ

We affirm that there is only one Savior and only one gospel, although there is a wide diversity of evangelistic approaches. We recognize that everyone has some knowledge of God through his general revelation in nature. But we deny that this can save, for people suppress the truth by their unrighteousness. We also reject as derogatory to Christ and the gospel every kind of syncretism and dialogue which implies that Christ speaks equally through all religions and ideologies. Jesus Christ, being himself the only God-man, who gave himself as the only ransom for sinners, is the only mediator between God and people. There is no other name by which we must be saved. All men and women are perishing because of sin, but God loves everyone, not wishing that any should perish but that all should repent. Yet those who reject Christ repudiate the joy of salvation and condemn themselves to eternal separation from God. To proclaim Jesus as "the Savior of the world" is not to affirm that all people are either automatically or ultimately saved, still less to affirm that all religions offer salvation in Christ. Rather it is to proclaim God's love for a world of sinners and to invite everyone to respond to him as Savior and Lord in the wholehearted personal commitment of repentance and faith. Jesus Christ has been exalted above every other name; we long for the day when every knee shall bow to him and every tongue shall confess him Lord. (Gal. 1:6–9; Rom. 1:18–32; 1 Tim. 2:5, 6; Acts 4:12; John 3:16–19; 2 Pet. 3:9; 2 Thess. 1:7–9; John 4:42; Matt. 11:28; Eph. 1:20, 21; Phil. 2:9–11)

4. The Nature of Evangelism

To evangelize is to spread the good news that Jesus Christ died for our sins and was raised from the dead according to the Scriptures, and that as the reigning Lord he now offers the forgiveness of sins and the liberating gifts of the Spirit to all who repent and believe. Our Christian presence in the world is indispensable to evangelism, and so is that kind of dialogue whose purpose is to listen sensitively in order to understand. But evangelism itself is the proclamation of the historical, biblical Christ as Savior and Lord, with a view to persuading people to come to him personally and so be reconciled

103

to God. In issuing the gospel invitation we have no liberty to conceal the cost of discipleship. Jesus still calls all who would follow him to deny themselves, take up their cross, and identify themselves with his new community. The results of evangelism include obedience to Christ, incorporation into his Church, and responsible service in the world. (1 Cor. 15:3, 4; Acts 2:32–39; John 20:21; 1 Cor. 1:23; 2 Cor. 4:5; 5:11, 20; Luke 14:25–33; Mark 8:34; Acts 2:40, 47; Mark 10:43–45)

5. Christian Social Responsibility

We affirm that God is both the Creator and the Judge of all men. We therefore should share his concern for justice and reconciliation throughout human society and for the liberation of men and women from every kind of oppression. Because men and women are made in the image of God, every person, regardless of race, religion, color, culture, class, sex, or age has an intrinsic dignity because of which he or she should be respected and served, not exploited. Here too we express penitence both for our neglect and for having sometimes regarded evangelism and social concern as mutually exclusive. Although reconciliation with other people is not reconciliation with God, nor is social action evangelism, nor is political liberation salvation, nevertheless we affirm that evangelism and socio-political involvement are both part of our Christian duty. For both are necessary expressions of our doctrines of God and man, our love for our neighbor, and our obedience to Jesus Christ. The message of salvation implies also a message of judgment upon every form of alienation, oppression, and discrimination, and we should not be afraid to denounce evil and injustice wherever they exist. When people receive Christ, they are born again into his kingdom and must seek not only to exhibit but also to spread its righteousness in the midst of an unrighteous world. The salvation we claim should be transforming us in the totality of our personal and social responsibilities. Faith without works is dead. (Acts 17:26, 31; Gen. 18:25; Isa. 1:17; Ps. 45:7; Gen. 1:26, 27; James 3:9; Lev. 19:18; Luke 6:27, 35; James 2:14–26; Joh. 3:3, 5; Matt. 5:20; 6:33; 2 Cor. 3:18; James 2:20)

6. The Church and Evangelism

We affirm that Christ sends his redeemed people into the world as the Father sent him, and that this calls for a similar deep and costly penetration of the world. We need to break out of our ecclesiastical ghettos and permeate non-Christian society. In the Church's mission of sacrificial service evangelism is primary. World evangelization requires the whole Church to take the whole gospel to the whole world. The Church is at the very center of God's cosmic purpose and is his appointed means of spreading the gospel. But a church which preaches the cross must itself be marked by the cross. It becomes a stumbling block to evangelism when it betrays the gospel or lacks a living faith in God, a genuine love for people, or scrupulous honesty in all things including promotion and finance. The church is the community of God's people rather than an institution, and must not be identified with any particular culture, social or political system, or human ideology. (John 17:18; 20:21; Matt. 28:19, 20; Acts 1:8; 20:27; Eph. 1:9, 10; 3:9–11; Gal. 6:14, 17; 2 Cor. 6:3, 4; 2 Tim. 2:19–21; Phil. 1:27)

7. Cooperation in Evangelism

We affirm that the Church's visible unity in truth is God's purpose. Evangelism also summons us to unity, because our oneness strengthens our witness, just as our disunity undermines our gospel of reconciliation. We recognize, however, that organizational unity may take many forms and does not necessarily forward evangelism. Yet we who share the same biblical faith should be closely united in fellowship, work, and witness. We confess that our testimony has sometimes been marred by a sinful individualism and needless duplication. We pledge ourselves to seek a deeper unity in truth, worship, holiness, and mission. We urge the development of regional and functional cooperation for the furtherance of the Church's mission, for strategic planning, for mutual encouragement, and for the sharing of resources and experience. (John 17:21, 23; Eph. 4:3, 4; John 13:35; Phil. 1:27; John 17:11–23)

8. Churches in Evangelistic Partnership

We rejoice that a new missionary era has dawned. The dominant role of western missions is fast disappearing. God is raising up from the younger churches a great new resource for world evangelization, and is thus demonstrating that the responsibility to evangelize belongs to the whole body of Christ. All churches should therefore be asking God and themselves what they should be doing both to reach their own area and to send missionaries to other parts of the world. A reevaluation of our missionary responsibility and role should be continuous. Thus a growing partnership of churches will develop and the universal character of Christ's Church will be more clearly exhibited. We also thank God for agencies which labor in Bible translation, theological education, the mass media, Christian literature, evangelism, missions, church renewal, and other specialist fields. They too should engage in constant self-examination to evaluate their effectiveness as part of the Church's mission. (Rom. 1:8; Phil. 1:5; 4:15; Acts 13:1–3; 1 Thess. 1:6–8)

9. The Urgency of the Evangelistic Task

More than 2,700 million people, which is more than two-thirds of all humanity, have yet to be evangelized. We are ashamed that so many have been neglected; it is a standing rebuke to us and to the whole Church. There is now, however, in many parts of the world an unprecedented receptivity to the Lord Jesus Christ. We are convinced that this is the time for churches and parachurch agencies to pray earnestly for the salvation of the unreached and to launch new efforts to achieve world evangelization. A reduction of foreign missionaries and money in an evangelized country may sometimes be necessary to facilitate the national church's growth in self-reliance and to release resources for unevangelized areas. Missionaries should flow ever more freely from and to all six continents in a spirit of humble service. The goal should be, by all available means and at the earliest possible time, that every person will have the opportunity to hear, understand, and to receive the good news. We cannot hope to attain this goal without sacrifice. All of us are shocked by the poverty of millions and disturbed by the injustices which cause it. Those of us who live in affluent circumstances accept our duty to develop a simple lifestyle in order to contribute more generously to both relief and evangelism. (John 9:4; Matt. 9:35–38;

Rom. 9:1–3; 1 Cor. 9:19–23; Mark 16:15; Isa. 58:6, 7; James 1:27; 2:1–9; Matt. 25:31–46; Acts 2:44, 45; 4:34, 35)

10. Evangelism and Culture

The development of strategies for world evangelization calls for imaginative pioneering methods. Under God, the result will be the rise of churches deeply rooted in Christ and closely related to their culture. Culture must always be tested and judged by Scripture. Because men and women are God's creatures, some of their culture is rich in beauty and goodness. Because they are fallen, all of it is tainted with sin and some of it is demonic. The gospel does not presuppose the superiority of any culture to another, but evaluates all cultures according to its own criteria of truth and righteousness, and insists on moral absolutes in every culture. Missions have all too frequently exported with the gospel an alien culture, and churches have sometimes been in bondage to culture rather than to Scripture. Christ's evangelists must humbly seek to empty themselves of all but their personal authenticity in order to become the servants of others, and churches must seek to transform and enrich culture, all for the glory of God. (Mark 7:8, 9, 13; Gen. 4:21, 22; 1 Cor. 9:19–23; Phil. 2:5–7; 2 Cor. 4:5)

11. Education and Leadership

We confess that we have sometimes pursued church growth at the expense of church depth, and divorced evangelism from Christian nurture. We also acknowledge that some of our missions have been too slow to equip and encourage national leaders to assume their rightful responsibilities. Yet we are committed to indigenous principles, and long that every church will have national leaders who manifest a Christian style of leadership in terms not of domination but of service. We recognize that there is a great need to improve theological education, especially for church leaders. In every nation and culture there should be an effective training program for pastors and laity in doctrine, discipleship, evangelism, nurture, and service. Such training programs should not rely on any stereotyped methodology but should be developed by creative local initiatives according to biblical standards. (Col. 1:27, 28; Acts 14:23; Tit. 1:5, 9; Mark 10:42–45; Eph. 4:11, 12)

12. Spiritual Conflict

We believe that we are engaged in constant spiritual warfare with the principalities and powers of evil, who are seeking to overthrow the Church and frustrate its task of world evangelization. We know our need to equip ourselves with God's armor and to fight this battle with the spiritual weapons of truth and prayer. For we detect the activity of our enemy, not only in false ideologies outside the Church, but also inside it in false gospels which twist Scripture and put people in the place of God. We need both watchfulness and discernment to safeguard the biblical gospel. We acknowledge that we ourselves are not immune to worldliness of thoughts and action, that is, to a surrender to secularism. For example, although careful studies of church growth, both numerical and spiritual, are right and valuable, we have sometimes neglected them. At other times, desirous to ensure a response to the gospel, we have compromised our message, manipulated our hearers through pressure techniques, and become unduly preoccupied with statistics or even dishonest in our use of them. All this is worldly. The Church must be in the world; the world must not be in the Church. (Eph. 6:12; 2 Cor. 4:3, 4; Eph. 6:11, 13–18; 2 Cor. 10:3–5; 1 John 2:18–26; 4:1–3; Gal. 1:6–9; 2 Cor. 2:17; 4:2; John 17:15)

13. Freedom and Persecution

It is the God-appointed duty of every government to secure conditions of peace, justice, and liberty in which the Church may obey God, serve the Lord Jesus Christ, and preach the gospel without interference. We therefore pray for the leaders of nations and call upon them to guarantee freedom of thought and conscience, and freedom to practice and propagate religion in accordance with the will of God and as set forth in The Universal Declaration of Human Rights. We also express our deep concern for all who have been unjustly imprisoned, and especially for those who are suffering for their testimony to the Lord Jesus. We promise to pray and work for their freedom. At the same time we refuse to be intimidated by their fate. God helping us, we too will seek to stand against injustice and to remain faithful to the gospel, whatever the cost. We do not forget the warnings of Jesus that persecution is inevitable. (1 Tim. 1:1–4, Acts 4:19; 5:29; Col. 3:24; Heb. 13:1–3; Luke 4:18; Gal. 5:11; 6:12; Matt. 5:10–12; John 15:18-21)

14. The Power of the Holy Spirit

We believe in the power of the Holy Spirit. The Father sent his Spirit to bear witness to his Son; without his witness ours is futile. Conviction of sin, faith in Christ, new birth, and Christian growth are all his work. Further, the Holy Spirit is a missionary spirit; thus evangelism should arise spontaneously from a Spirit-filled church. A church that is not a missionary church is contradicting itself and quenching the Spirit. Worldwide evangelization will become a realistic possibility only when the Spirit renews the Church in truth and wisdom, faith, holiness, love, and power. We therefore call upon all Christians to pray for such a visitation of the sovereign Spirit of God that all his fruit may appear in all his people and that all his gifts may enrich the body of Christ. Only then will the whole church become a fit instrument in his hands, that the whole earth may hear his voice. (1 Cor. 2:4; John 15:26, 27; 16:8–11; 1 Cor. 12:3; John 3:6–8; 2 Cor. 3:18; John 7:37–39; 1 Thess. 5:19; Acts 1:8; Ps. 85:4–7; 67:1–3; Gal. 5:22, 23; 1 Cor. 12:4–31; Rom. 12:3–8)

15. The Return of Christ

We believe that Jesus Christ will return personally and visibly, in power and glory, to consummate his salvation and his judgment. This promise of his coming is a further spur to our evangelism, for we remember his words that the gospel must first be preached to all nations. We believe that the interim period between Christ's ascension and return is to be filled with the mission of the people of God, who have no liberty to stop before the end. We also remember his warning that false Christs and false prophets will arise as precursors of the final Antichrist. We therefore reject as a proud, self-confident dream the notion that people can ever build a utopia on earth. Our Christian confidence is that God will perfect his kingdom, and we look forward with eager anticipation to that day, and to the new heaven and earth in which righteousness

109

will dwell and God will reign forever. Meanwhile, we rededicate ourselves to the service of Christ and of people in joyful submission to his authority over the whole of our lives. (Mark 14:62; Heb. 9:28; Mark 13:10; Acts 1:8–11; Matt. 28:20; Mark 13:21–23; John 2:18; 4:1–3; Luke 12:32; Rev. 21:1–5; 2 Pet. 3:13; Matt. 28:18)

Conclusion

Therefore, in the light of this our faith and our resolve, we enter into a solemn covenant with God and with each other to pray, to plan, and to work together for the evangelization of the whole world. We call upon others to join us. May God help us by his grace and for his glory to be faithful to this our covenant! Amen, Alleluia!

This is the new global Christian reality! This, rather than tired old debates on the culture wars is where evangelical Christianity is at: African, Latin American, Asian, growing, dynamic, expanding. Forget what you read in Western secular newspapers. *This* is evangelicalism in the twenty-first century and where it will be, I suspect, for some time to come.

Five

Trials and Tribulations

One day Jesus is coming back. That is something believed in by Christians of all different stripes and denominations, and by every evangelical Christian regardless of whatever other views they might have.

So far so good—but now it gets a bit more complicated! For while evangelicals all believe in what we call the second coming—when Jesus returns to earth to wind up history—the *mechanism* of that event is something on which there is no consensus within evangelical Christianity. (In general, nonevangelical Christians usually believe in only two of the views I will present, so for these people what follows is likely to be as much of a mystery as it is for secular readers. For many British readers, the whole debate will probably be somewhat of a puzzle, since, although British evangelicals are as divided on this issue as their fellow evangelicals in other countries, it has never reached the prominence within British evangelicalism as it has elsewhere, notably in the United States; some denominations, such as the Assemblies of God, even have their interpretation of eschatology in their statements of faith.)

But within evangelical Christianity this remains a hot issue for some, and it has potentially major *political* implications, especially in relation to US foreign policy in Israel.

In the past I have always tried to avoid writing about what Christians call *eschatology*, or what is popularly know as the *end times*. This is because, as we shall discover, it is a doctrine much discussed and argued over among evangelicals themselves, sometimes giving the impression that there are so many potential views that they make denominational differences pale into the shade. There is bound to be someone whose views will be upset, and that is always a shame.

However, the diverging doctrines of the end times have achieved mammoth international publicity, partly through the astronomic sales success of Tim LaHaye and Jerry Jenkins's Left Behind series of novels (well over 60 million sold in just a few years), and because of the influence evangelicals held during the eight years of the George W. Bush presidency, especially since President Bush was known to be sympathetic to one form of eschatology.[1]

So this time there is no escape!

Let us start by noting something important: *there really are lots of different views on this subject among evangelicals.* This is something almost entirely ignored by the secular press, who have picked the one most followed in the United States as being representative of evangelicals altogether, both in North America and worldwide. It is also true to say that while many evangelicals do hold their particular view of eschatology deeply, and would even go so far as to say that it *ought* to be the view that all evangelicals *should* hold, they would never go so far to say you *have* to hold it in order to call yourself an evangelical.

Eschatological Views

What, then, are these different theories?

    a. amillennialism
    b. postmillennialism
    c. historic premillennialism
    d. dispensational pretribulation premillennialism
    e. varieties of (d), or post-tribulation premillennialism

I should add that there is a less-than-serious 1960s version, nick-named *panmillennialism*; American preacher and writer R. T. Kendall jokingly said to a group of Christians in London that it is called by that name because its adherents know that all these different views will one day pan together in the end.

So let us start at the beginning, where all evangelical (and other Christian) views agree: *Jesus Christ is coming back*. There was a first coming, what we celebrate as Christmas, followed by the ascension, when Jesus went back to heaven shortly after the resurrection, and one day he will come back again. History will then end, there will be a last judgment, and Christians will spend eternity in heaven with God.

What, therefore, is the millennium? It is here that the differences begin.

We all know what a literal millennium is—a thousand-year period, of the kind that began in 2001. For Christians things are not necessarily so simple, depending upon your eschatology.

Revelation 20 mentions a *thousand-year* period. It is principally upon this chapter that the views of Christians, and of evangelicals in particular, tend to diverge. What is this thousand-year period? Is it *symbolic* (the amillennial view)? Or is it *literal* (the premillennial and postmillennial views)? And, just to make life exciting for the perplexed, *if* it is literal, *when* does it take place? It is on the latter point that the premillennial and postmillennial views diverge.

One problem in looking at this subject is that believers of the last three views in the list above hold that their version, the correct one, is a doctrine with antecedents in the first four centuries of the Christian church. But concerning those who believe in either of the other two interpretations, any form of *premillennialism* does not really predate the nineteenth century, when what is called *dispensationalism* came into the church, especially through the writings of one of the founders of the Plymouth Brethren, the British thinker J. N. Darby, though his followers would argue otherwise.

So premillennialism is either the correct interpretation of the Bible *or* a nineteenth-century invention whose existence has been read back into history by its modern proponents. And finally, just to make life more interesting, premillennialists divide according to whether they hold to dispensationalism, which teaches that there are different *ages*, one of which (here most evangelicals do agree) is the time between Christ's ascension and his return, and the other, which dispensationalists teach, is a *literal* millennium, whether pre- or post-.

(I am here omitting some of the more complex eschatological doctrines, such as chialism, preterism, and similar theories, which really need specialist knowledge to unpack in full. But we will need to consider the *tribulation*, especially when looking at the dispensationalist varieties of premillennial doctrine. We also need to look at views of the *Antichrist*, with people from Nero to Saddam Hussein, Napoleon to Adolf Hitler, being described as the Antichrist by different Christians throughout the centuries.)

Having made the necessary cautions, we can begin to look at what these different doctrines teach and attempt to see where they fit into the history of the church. Then we can conclude by looking at how dispensationalist premillennialism fits into US foreign policy, since its proponents are far more important (during a Republican presidency, at least) in terms of lobbying for American support for Israel than any mythical "Jewish lobby," in whose existence the media might want us to believe.

Amillennialism

Put simply, *amillennialism* is the doctrine that says that any thousand-year period referred to in Revelation 20 is *symbolic* and not literal. Thus, in essence, the *millennium* is the time in-between the ascension and when Christ returns at the last judgment to end history and create a new heaven and a new earth, with all who follow Jesus as their Savior and Lord going to spend eternity with him in heaven. For amillennialists, it is as straightforward as that.

This means that what the Bible calls *tribulation* is the ongoing life of the church in *all* ages. Christians were savagely persecuted in the first centuries of the church, they were appallingly treated and often martyred by Communist countries in the twentieth century, and today Christians continue to be persecuted—and not just in the Islamic world where Christianity is often forbidden, but in places like India, where extremist Hindus create new Christian martyrs all the time. As for the

Antichrist, such anti-Christian figures exist all the time (such as the names we saw earlier), and will continue to exist, persecuting God's people, until the end of time.

The advantage of the amillennial view is that all of Revelation applies to all Christians at all times throughout the entire history of the church. What we see are not *literal* figures, but *archetypes,* and we can see that whatever happens to God's people, the church, however appalling the persecution might be, however powerful antichrist figures may seem, God's will always prevails. Jesus is with his people, and one day he will return and judge the world. Nothing, however heinous, can defeat God, which is a source of comfort to Christians down the ages. It means that Revelation (and the similar passages in the Old Testament book of Daniel) is not some code to be cracked or some prophecy of distant times yet to occur, but a book that is profoundly relevant and comprehensible to all Christians of all ages.

It is for this reason that your author is amillennial; this is the interpretation that makes the most obvious sense, and it is one that can be as similarly understood by Christians being persecuted in the sixteenth century as by their spiritual family in the twenty-first.

Amillennialism is also, interestingly enough, the same view held by the Roman Catholic Church. In this the Catholic Church goes back a long way—it was the view of the great fifth-century theologian, St. Augustine of Hippo, a writer and thinker who today is revered by Protestants as well as Catholics, especially among evangelicals in the Reformed, or Presbyterian, wing of the church. But it was also the view of the great Protestant Reformers of the Reformation period, and of its founder Martin Luther, and likewise, in more recent times, of people such as Dr. D. Martyn Lloyd-Jones. So amillennialism has ancient roots and also strong present-day evangelical adherents.

Postmillennialism

Not all Reformers held to the amillennial view however, most notably the French-born Geneva leader, John Calvin. Their view, which was also that of the Pilgrim fathers and many of the early American Puritans, is called *postmillennialism.* It is what one might call the cheerful view, and one I would love to believe in if only I could be convinced. Many in the Reformed theological world today are postmillennial, notably people like Iain Murray, author of *The Puritan Hope*, leading British evangelical and writer Sir Fred Catherwood, and, to the astonishment of many in Reformed circles, the late John Wimber, founder of the charismatic Vineyard movement of churches, and someone who regularly bought copies of *The Puritan Hope* in gigantic batches.[2]

This view is optimistic in that it argues that Christ's second coming and the last judgment come *after* Christians rule the entire world for a thousand-year period—that is, Christ's return is *post* the millennium, the rule of the saints, God's Christian people on earth. Some postmillennialists argue that things will temporarily get very bad between the end of the millennium and Christ's arrival, but that Satan's attempt to derail the rule of God's people will be defeated when Jesus comes back.

As we will see, premillennialists think things are getting worse as we approach the last days. Postmillennialists, by contrast, think they are getting better! And for natural optimists, statistics are on their side. Over half the people who have ever lived are alive now—so great has been the population explosion of the past one hundred or so years—and Christianity is blossoming exponentially in all parts of the world, as never before. Africa is on its way to becoming a predominantly Christian continent, and persecution has increased the size of the church in China by at least 4,000 percent if not far more than that. Naturally such statistics are grist to the mill of many a postmillennial evangelical!

There is also little doubt historically that much of the optimism that characterized the founding fathers of the United States stems from what Murray is correct to call the *Puritan hope.* Their sense of expectation and the feeling that they were bringing in God's righteous kingdom to the new colonies is closely related to their eschatological outlook. One can say that in that sense, the United States was founded upon postmillennial optimism.

However, if this view is a correct one, the rule of the saints is not with us yet. Some four hundred years after the Pilgrims set sail for their new Promised Land, countless millions more people have become Christians, and in parts of the world in which Christianity was unknown before, but the rule of the saints globally is still ahead of us, if it is coming at all. *Spiritually* things are indeed increasingly encouraging, but the *political* fulfillment of the dreams of the Puritans has yet to arrive.

Premillennialism

So now we come to the view that has gained the most notoriety in recent years and has been a cover story even in the secular press: *premillennialism.*

Here one needs to say that there are in fact several subsets of premillennialism, not all of which agree with each other.

One of them, *historic premillennialism,* for example, does not hold to dispensationalism (the view that we are divided into different church ages between Christ's first and second coming). This view is therefore closer in spirit to the first two we have seen, who similarly reject such a doctrine. Perhaps the best-known holder of this view in the United States is the Californian preacher John MacArthur, who originally came from a dispensationalist background but who theologically has now moved into the Reformed wing of evangelical Christianity. (Many a North American Calvinist evangelical is or has been a follower of historic premillennialism, most notably Francis Schaeffer.)

However, most premillennialists are firmly in the dispensational camp: they believe that between the ascension of Jesus that we read about in the book of Acts and his second coming at the end of time—what they call the last days—God has divided history into discrete chunks of time, or what they call *dispensations.*

One of these will be after what they call the *tribulation,* a period of Satanic predominance on earth, in which anyone still believing in Jesus will be most savagely persecuted. This era will take place after an event they call the *rapture,* when all Christians living upon earth will suddenly, dramatically, and unexpectedly be taken straight to heaven; Christians alive at the rapture will not die in the normal way but be transported directly heavenward.

This is a view that, perhaps to the surprise of many, originated not in the United States but in Britain, and in particular with British Plymouth Brethren leader J. N. Darby. Most Brethren in Britain still hold to this doctrine as part of their basis of faith—my paternal grandmother as a child would regularly rush into her parents' bedroom at night, if she could not sleep, to check whether her parents had been raptured, and thus leaving her behind. Many other British evangelicals, notably those in the Pentecostal Assemblies of God, also hold strongly to this doctrine. It is therefore one with strong British antecedents and not some strange flowering of belief arising in the United States.

Nevertheless, it is in the United States where this doctrine is most powerfully held, not least because of the marginal notes in the Scofield Reference Bible (owned by many generations of American evangelicals) that explain the relevant passages in the book of Revelation in a premillennial way.

Just to make life interesting, premillennial dispensationalists are themselves divided on exactly where in the scheme of things the rapture and tribulation take place. With Christians raptured, non-Christians are, in that sense, "left behind." The Left Behind series has made this view known worldwide. However, the LaHaye/Jenkins view is in fact only one version of dispensational belief. They have the Christians all raptured *before* the tribulation, or what is thus called *pretribulationism*. Other equally strong premillennial dispensationalists hold that Christians will be raptured in the *middle* of the tribulation, hence their name *midtribulationists*. So while the novels have by now influenced the eschatology of millions, strictly speaking theirs is only one of a series of options even within the premillennial school of belief.

So, you can be a *midtribulationist dispensationalist premillennialist.*

All varieties of premillennial views do agree that when the tribulation finishes, Christ will come back and rule on earth for a thousand years. Therefore all the great events of Revelation take place *before* or *pre-* the millennium, hence the name. Not only that but the political events that they argue are predicted in Revelation—the Antichrist, the Beast, wars between kings of the North and South—are all *literal* future events, and relate, in some way or another, to countries that may well exist now. Mikhail Gorbachev's prominent birthmark on his bald patch excited many for a long while (they believed that the USSR was the kingdom of the North, while it existed) and likewise the late Saddam Hussein's rule over an area that included the site of the original Babylon exercised many premillennialists for some while before 2003.

For many nonevangelicals reading this, or for many evangelicals outside of the United States, much of this chapter might seem like the twenty-first-century equivalent of the medieval debate of how many angels could dance on the head of a pin, which was taken very seriously by major scholars at the time.

Indeed, in many parts of the evangelical world outside of the United States, the reaction to the medieval scholastic debate would be a view that would gather much sympathy. We evangelicals hold all our views strongly—on the mode of baptism, the nature of church government, the relationship between church and state, the method of evangelism, and much else besides. But, as we saw in chapter 1, there are core doctrines in which *all* evangelical Christians believe, regardless of denominational affiliation and interpretation, and of how much we might disagree, even vigorously, on much else.

Globally, therefore, evangelicals usually find themselves agreeing on what Luther called the essential matters, and diverging on what he described as *matters indifferent*. Evangelical gatherings will thus have Baptists, Presbyterians, Methodists, and Episcopalians all mixing happily cheek by jowl, united in the gospel however strong their divisions on other matters. This is also true for large swathes of American evangelicalism, who hold their several views of the millennium as deeply as those on, say, baptism or church government, but nonetheless place their eschatology in the second of Luther's two categories.

However, in the early twentieth century, many premillennial evangelicals added their particular interpretation of the millennium to the set of *core* beliefs that you *must* have in order to call yourself an evangelical at all. This was unfortunate in many ways, but also understandable in the particular context of America at the time. The reason is simple. There were amillennial evangelicals and also theological liberals who were amillennial, and *postmillennial* evangelicals and also theologically liberal followers of that view, but *there were no theologically liberal premillennialists.*

So being, say, postmillennialist, did not guarantee that you were evangelical in your core doctrines; many liberals, who rejected the foundational doctrines of Scripture, for example, could also be postmillennialists. The same applied to amillennialists.

However, as there were no liberal premillennialists, if somebody were premillennialist, according to this argument, he *had* to be an evangelical. So in order to make 101 percent sure that somebody was a fellow evangelical, many dispensationalists in the United States insisted that to be evangelical you had to be premillennial as well, since that insistence would automatically exclude theological liberals. And, since within the context of evangelicalism *in the United States* that still left a huge number of evangelicals within the fold, that is the pattern that persisted and remains true of many denominations in the United States even today.

Politics

The strong prevalence of premillennial theology has also had profound political implications, especially after the rise of the religious right in the United States after the 1970s. This is because of the premillennial belief that the resurrection of the Jewish state—the creation of Israel as an independent nation in 1948—is the fulfillment of much biblical prophecy. In fact one could say that the birth of Israel, and that nation's continued existence under heavy external attack, has done more to recruit for premillennialism than even the legendary Scofield Bible.

Consequently, American evangelicals of dispensationalist disposition are today some of the most zealous supporters of the state of Israel, since they see its very creation as part of God's work and as an answer to prophecy. This means that when there is a Republican government—especially one, as under George W. Bush, with a president who is dispensationalist himself—the evangelical lobby on foreign affairs, and on Israel in particular, is massively influential. It is this truth that makes nonsense of the idea in the secular media of a *Jewish* lobby and its mythic power. While millions of American Jews do indeed support the state of Israel and do also lobby for it, electorally speaking the evangelical lobby for Israel is many times larger and far more important in terms of mobilizing the Republican Party base, not just in presidential elections but in those for Congress as well.

(Victoria Clark's book *Allies for Armageddon*, where she describes evangelicals as being *Christian Zionists*, gives much insight into how this theology began not in the United States but in Britain, long before

www.maf-uk.org

Visit our website for all the
latest news for prayer

Please pray especially for:

- Our ability to bring help,
  hope and healing in
  emergency situations
- Stamina and good health
  in areas of staff shortage
- Recruitment of senior-level
  staff
- Provision of resources
  during the global recession

Thank you for praying for
the work of MAF

Flying for Life

Mission Aviation Fellowship
Castle Hill Avenue, Folkestone CT20 2TN
29 Canal Street Glasgow G4 0AD
Telephone: 0845 850 9505
Email: supporter.relations@maf-uk.org
Website: www.maf-uk.org

Registered charity in England and Wales (1064598)
and in Scotland (SC039107)

Mission Aviation Fellowship

Home | Who we are | Where we work | Who we help | News | Get involved | Co

Mission Aviation Fellowship

Spin-offs	Passion for the unreached

'Sometimes MAF flights have spin-offs that you don't expect,' says missionary John Rowse in Tanzania
Read more about his remarkable story

MAF flights in Kenya enable evangelistic meetings - and leads to much rejoicing
read more

Email a friend | Print this page | Site map | Privacy | Terms & Conditions | Accessibilit

Why not visit our website

www.maf-uk.org

- Discover the latest news
- Find out where we fly
- Book a speaker
- Sign up for enewsletters
- Order our range of resources
- Check out our overseas vacancies
- Get involved

Flying for Life

Israel's creation, and that historically speaking, *British* Christian support for a Jewish homeland created the atmosphere that led the United Kingdom to create what was then Palestine as a homeland for persecuted Jews, in the Balfour Declaration of 1917. Just as J. N. Darby was British, we in the United Kingdom should remember that while "Christian Zionism" is now a predominantly American phenomenon, it is firmly one with powerful British antecedents.)

Most Israelis, surrounded by hostile Arab neighbors, are delighted to accept support from wherever it comes. If American evangelicals mobilize opinion in favor of Israel, they will take it. However, some religiously observant Israeli Jews have realized that all this support comes at a theological price, namely that most premillennial Americans (and those who hold similar views outside the United States) believe that the creation of Israel does not only bring forward the last days, but that Israel is also God's specified place *for the Jews to convert to Christianity*, to realize, during the time when they are "left behind" on earth before the second coming, that Jesus really is the awaited Jewish Messiah, and that Israeli Jews will therefore convert *en masse* to Christian faith during the horrors of the tribulation.

Needless to say, this is not good news for the *Israeli* religious right, who, for example, do not allow the right of return of Jews to Israel to *Messianic Jews*—that is people of ethnic Jewish ancestry who have converted in Britain, the United States, and elsewhere to Christianity and who regard Jesus as the already come Messiah. This is a paradox, of course: it is hard for Messianic Jews to live in Israel itself, since the consensus of Israeli opinion is that you cannot be both Jewish and Christian at the same time.

And just a thought on the enormous Jewish population of the United States: is it a coincidence that the world's largest concentration of God's Old Covenant people is in one of the most Christian countries on earth, certainly the most actively Christian in the West? Nearly all the premillennial versions of prophecy leave out the United States. Europe has a far stronger role, as any reader of the LaHaye novels knows; this bears no resemblance to geopolitical realities at all, with countries such as the United States, China, Brazil, and India all forecast to be the superpowers of the twenty-first century. *But* if there will be a spiritual movement

121

of Jews toward Jesus as Messiah—a thought abhorrent to Orthodox and liberal Jews alike but a fervent prayer of New Testament writer St. Paul, who was born a Jew—then perhaps the presence of millions of Jews in the United States might just be part of that fulfillment, and not the *political* existence of the state of Israel.

Well, that is just a thought!

However, all this—the success of the Left Behind series and the strong Christian Zionist lobby for Israel—has put the pretribulation premillennial dispensationalist interpretation of Scripture firmly on the map, and on international consciousness (even in the secular press itself).

Lest people outside the United States sneer, it is important to say that this interpretation has been influential in Britain as well, especially because of the attitude of its followers toward the European Union. When it looked briefly as if the European Community (as it then was) would have *ten* member states, many a sermon was preached warning that the EC would be like the dreaded ten hills predicted in Revelation. In particular, those Protestants of a more militantly anti-Catholic inclination reminded us all regularly that the founding treaty that established the original EC was the Treaty of Rome, and there was a brief period when the borders of the EC and that of the original Roman Empire in the West were not dissimilar. (Now the EU is well beyond any ancient Roman borders and has considerably more than ten members, including many majority Protestant states. The real problem in spiritual terms is not Catholic domination but the sheer strength of godless secular materialism, which is as rampant in formerly Protestant states as well as Catholic or Orthodox. As we have seen elsewhere in this book, secularization theory may have been proved false in the United States, Africa, and in many other parts of the world, but it is alas very accurate when applied to Europe.)

We must remember, however, that this is not the sole premillennial interpretation of eschatology, with historic premillennialism and midtribulationism taking a very different view of the tribulation than the one made famous in the recent novels. Then, quite apart from these views, there are the postmillennial and amillennial interpretations, with their *very* different interpretations of the last times.

Social Influence

Premillennialism had, for a long time, a devastating effect on evangelical engagement with society, especially after the Great Reversal at the end of the nineteenth and early twentieth centuries. (Here it should be said that premillennialist evangelicals like Francis Schaeffer are strong exceptions to this, since his teaching, during his period of greatest influence in the 1950s to 1970s, was that evangelicals *should* be involved in influencing the society in which God has put them.) The tendency of many premillennialists to say that society does not matter, because they will not be present during the tribulation, has been a cause of serious concern.

This attitude is, one can argue, a result of the premillennial doctrine of the rapture. Many evangelicals believed that if Christians were not going to be part of the end times—since they would have been raptured to heaven—then there was no urgency to fight for beneficial social change. Obviously it was not as simple as this, but the effect was quite detrimental to society. Whereas in the nineteenth century evangelicals were at the forefront of social improvement—Wilberforce and Lord Shaftesbury in England, the antislavery activists in the United States (who, we should not forget, included Charles Finney, the evangelist)—in much of the twentieth century there was a strong tendency to leave such activity to theological liberals, and for evangelicals to retreat into their own world, emerging only to evangelize. And Shaftesbury, it should be remembered, was one of the earliest supporters of evangelical lobbying for a Jewish homeland, decades before the state of Israel was even contemplated, let alone made a reality. So historically, active social concern for the poor and underprivileged and belief in some kind of premillennial theology/support for Israel have been far from incompatible.

Now in the twenty-first century there are encouraging signs that the Great Reversal is over, and that evangelicals in both Britain and the United States are becoming involved in caring for their neighbor, working in the inner cities, and campaigning not just on hot button issues of private morality but on matters such as human rights, the environment, and overseas development. So the introverted years in which eschatology turned evangelicals away from their neighbor are becoming, we can trust, increasingly something of the past.

That is not to say that dispensationalist pretribulation premillennialism is less potent in the United States—it may even be increasing—but we can say that the connection between holding that view and social inaction is quite possibly diminishing. Secular journalists such as Nicholas Kristof of the *New York Times* and Matthew Parris of the London *Times* are noticing the beneficial effects in Africa, and in crisis areas such as Darfur in particular, of evangelicals in the West, and so the reputation that evangelical Christianity had in the nineteenth century as being made up of people who care might be slowly on the way back.[3]

Does all this matter? For many of those who hold their own particular views, it matters a great deal! Is it as important as core evangelical beliefs such as the divinity of Jesus or the all-sufficiency of Christ's work upon the cross (something with which Protestants have all agreed among themselves since the Reformation)? I would argue no, although many evangelicals would think otherwise. But knowing that the end will come is, all evangelicals would agree, a wonderful encouragement to holiness, since who wants to be sinning the moment of Christ's actual return? All of us know he is returning, even if we differ on exactly *how*.

We can therefore end this chapter on eschatology on a positive note. And as for which of the many versions of the last days/end times will prove accurate, we should remember the clear command of Jesus Christ not to be obsessed by these things, but to concentrate on the task that we have *now*.

Six

The Minefield: A Survey of Evangelical Politics

The religious right—we've all heard of them, haven't we?

How many have also heard of the *religious left*, since they too exist in the United States and have been producing books since the 1970s? Up until recent times, they had been virtually unheard of in Britain and the wider world, until Prime Minister Gordon Brown wrote a preface for Jim Wallis's book, *God's Politics*, a work that also became compulsory reading for American Democrats desperate for evangelical votes in the 2008 presidential election.[1]

And, what is more to the point, should there really be a religious right or religious left at all? Should evangelicals be thought of as some kind of vast bloc vote, to be wooed when there is an election on, but otherwise, as many evangelicals in the United States find to their chagrin, taken for granted and essentially ignored otherwise?

And how does the evangelical connection to politics tie in with the great evangelical issues of the past—the abolition of the slave trade and of child labor in factories in Britain, and the abolition of slavery itself in the United States? What would the effect have been if, say, all the evangelicals in 1800 were Whigs, not both Whigs and Tories (and many of no fixed political abode)? How successful would Wilberforce and Shaftesbury have been if all their fellow evangelicals had been lumped together as following only one of the two major political parties in Britain in the nineteenth century?

Finally, is the stereotype in the United States accurate—that when you think of evangelicals, you *automatically* also think of Republicans? (And not just of Republicans, but of those on the far right of that party, and of people who have not just strong views on moral issues, but who are firmly anti-intellectual as well.)

There are numerous clichés when it comes to looking at evangelicals in the United States, some of which are scare-mongering nonsense on the part of liberal media intellectuals in both Britain and America who want to make our flesh creep, and some, alas, that are self-inflicted injuries which we evangelicals could, if we took any trouble, easily avoid.

Although I am British, I am married to an American and I have talked about the issue of politics with evangelical friends now for over thirty years. I have seen major shifts, from the years of President Carter when evangelicals seemed to be Democrats, to the present, where meeting an evangelical Democrat is increasingly rare.

In order to write this sensitively—as a British evangelical commenting on another country—I interviewed off the record a leading young evangelical thinker connected to one of the major Midwest seminaries. I also read a book by another, older professor at Calvin College, Steve Monsma, titled *Healing for a Broken World.*[2] Much of what follows is indebted to these two sources, though I should add that, as always, what follows is very much my own interpretation and is the result of more than thirty years of discussion with politically aware fellow evangelicals in the United States.

When talking to people about this book, one of the Caribbean's leading Christians told me that many evangelicals in the Two-thirds World found the description *evangelical* a highly embarrassing one during the presidency of George W. Bush, who was, perhaps, the highest profile evangelical, at least so far as the secular media were concerned, during his eight years in office.

That people in other countries should not want to use an entirely bib-lical term about themselves because of the public failures of an elected American politician shows how much the United States still dominates the thought patterns of the world in which we live, and how we still see the globe through what is essentially an American terminological perspective. For, as we have seen elsewhere in this book, what is true of the United States is not necessarily true of the rest of the world, the state of evangelical Christianity fully included.

I was also fascinated, in visiting the United States during the Bush presidency, with how deeply disillusioned many theologically *and politically* conservative Americans were with President Bush, espe-cially those, surely not without coincidence, who had close links with evangelicals in other countries. They could see the way in which the policies and (they felt, not just me) the sheer ineptitude of the Bush Administration were doing massive damage to the reputation of the United States in the wider world. They were embarrassed as Republi-cans, as evangelicals, and as patriotic Americans.

However, Bush is no longer president. And many of the major leaders of the Christian Coalition, of the religious right, are no longer around either. Jerry Falwell, the founder of Liberty University, has died, as has James Kennedy of Coral Ridge Presbyterian Church in Florida, some-one not so well known in Britain but a senior figure on the religious right in the United States. Similarly, James Dobson of Focus on the Family, whose radio show was listened to by millions in the United States up until his retirement from it in 2010 (and whose books on child rearing have been read by thousands in Britain) has retired; his is another major voice linking evangelicalism to the Republican Party that will no longer be heard.

So at the same time as the Bush Administration ends, a consider-able generational shift is occurring that will make the nature of the religious right change—regardless of political events, such as Barack Obama becoming President of the United States.

No one, my younger source advised me, is taking up the mantle in quite the way that these people did, except perhaps Al Mohler, the head of Southern Baptist Theological Seminary in Louisville, Kentucky, someone controversial in his own denomination for trying to reintroduce Reformed theology back into the Southern Baptist Convention. It is interesting, for instance, that the new pastor of Coral Ridge, a grandson of Billy Graham, is a man in his thirties who is theologically conservative, but is highly skeptical of the efficacy of preaching politics from the pulpit.

So many preachers of large churches in the United States are doctrinal conservatives; but while they are almost certainly voting Republican in private, they no longer see it as their job to preach partisan politics in their Sunday sermons.

For one of the biggest evangelical churches in the United States, this has always been the case: Grace Community Church, lead by John F. MacArthur Jr., in the famous San Fernando Valley in California. Once when I visited Focus on the Family (when it was still in California), Dobson was rewarding staff members who had picketed abortion clinics and in some cases had been arrested in the process. I then heard John MacArthur preach the following Sunday, making it clear that illegal action was not an option for Christians, and that in a democracy, persuasion rather than violent action was the best way for Christians to win people over to the rightness of their cause.

MacArthur is an American preacher whose message is heard as far as Britain and India, and who feels that preaching should be Bible-based and not culturally specific: hence, one imagines, his receptive audience in India as well as the United States. His book *Why Government Can't Save You* might go a little too far in the other direction (Christians in the pew can do a lot to change society, as Wilberforce showed us), but it does make very plain from Scripture that the pulpit is for proclaiming salvation in Jesus Christ, not a partisan political diatribe that links the eternal truths of the Christian faith to manmade human solutions.[3] MacArthur may be controversial within evangelicalism—he tells things as he sees them! But on this issue, on the political neutrality of the pulpit, he has proved to have been ahead of his time, as the debacle of the Bush years has woken many evangelical pastors up to the dangers of linking the gospel to fallible partisan ends, even though many of them still vote Republican *in private*. (This is a theme that Monsma also deals with, as we shall see later, as it is relevant to what others would call *American exceptionalism*.)

Rethinking Evangelicalism's Involvement in Society

Likewise, many American evangelicals are now aware that there are a lot of other issues out there, other than what has hitherto been *the* great litmus test, abortion, the issue that has mobilized evangelicals and Catholics alike since the passing of Roe vs. Wade in the Supreme Court back in the 1970s. The situation in 2010, as of my writing this, is still in flux or under discussion, with the Obama presidency still brand new. Since it is important not to date this book, I will not go into great detail about Obama himself, other than to say that when it comes to his view of evangelicals, the jury is still out.

One group hopes that since he is a professing Christian—albeit of a different theological stripe—many of the issues to which evangelicals have recently woken up can be dealt with, and very effectively, under his presidency. These are matters such as global and domestic poverty, aid to developing countries, the pandemic AIDS crisis (especially in Africa), human rights, social justice, and the environment.

This is not to say that abortion—what one leader called "the holocaust of our generation"— no longer matters. But evangelicals are now not *just* concerned about abortion, which was the impression they gave until recently, but abortion *and* social justice, or abortion *and* protecting the environment.

Therefore, some evangelical leaders have been willing, for example, to join the new President's council of pastors. One of these is Joel Hunter, a pastor of a large church in Florida, and who, to my recent astonishment, received a warm write-up in Britain's *Guardian* newspaper, not usually a publication remotely friendly to evangelicals of any kind.

Also on the council is Jim Wallis, of the Sojourners community in Washington, DC. This is not surprising—he is in many ways as associated with Democrats as people of an earlier generation, such as Pat Robertson, were with Republicans. Wallis is not alone in his affiliation: other evangelicals have been overt in their support for Democrats in recent years, albeit nowhere near the size of those who have supported Republicans.

So Wallis being on the council is not surprising, but someone more overtly theologically conservative such as Hunter is interesting. But as my informant told me, whether they stay on the council is contingent on whether President Obama is seen to be neutral on the abortion issue—pro-choice but not *overzealously* pro-choice. On this we will have to wait and see.

Another evangelical leader to note is Rick Warren, pastor of a huge megachurch in California called Saddleback. He is also the author of the most successful Christian book in decades, *The Purpose Driven Life*, which has sold millions of copies around the world.[4]

The secular media have called Warren the new Billy Graham, which is a tribute to his influence but is perhaps misleading as no one today has quite the same standing that Graham did in his early pioneering years back in the 1950s and 1960s. Nonetheless, Warren is enormously influential; only he, I've been told, had the clout to invite both Obama and McCain to his church to debate the major ethical and theological issues of the 2008 presidential campaign. Giving the invocation at the Obama inaugural in 2009 is itself an iconic moment: an evangelical at a *Democrat's* swearing-in, and this despite howls of rage from ultraliberal groups on the Democratic left, who dislike Warren's stand against gay marriage in the 2008 California plebiscite on that controversial subject.

As I was told, in 2004 Warren had been, like so many evangelical pastors of the time, someone who urged his followers to vote Republican. Then he discovered the error of that public proclamation, and he also found that other causes existed (his focus is on AIDS and poverty in Africa). So while he might well privately still vote Republican—Obama's remark in Saddleback that an issue such as abortion was "above my pay grade" did not go down too well among evangelicals—the fact that he had Obama more than once in his church shows that the spirit of automatic partisanship of many evangelical pulpits is now over.

So much for the issues of the moment—what about the deeper, *spiritual* dimension of how evangelicals in the United States are rethinking how best to act in future? Here we can turn to the matters Monsma raises in his book. *Healing for a Broken World* was endorsed both by Chuck Colson, famous for his involvement in the Watergate scandal, known for being on the political right, and praised for his book *Born Again*,[5] and by Ron Sider, president of Evangelicals for Social Action and on the political left. Sider is less familiar to the media, but he has been well known in evangelical Labor Party and Liberal Democrat circles in Britain for decades, notably for his book *Rich Christians in an Age of Hunger.*[6]

By way of introduction to Monsma's book, let me ask, why do many *American* evangelicals think as they do about certain issues?

Monsma addresses this question, but, your author being an historian, I want to take it further back than he does, back to the self-image the United States had when it began centuries ago. For this I rely on an excellent book by University of Pennsylvania history professor Walter McDougall, *Promised Land, Crusader State.*[7] This work is in fact about US foreign policy, but McDougall correctly realizes that to understand how the United States relates to the rest of the world, and also how it sees itself, you have to understand the *religious* underpinning of the American state.

My wife, being from Virginia, a state that was founded not for godly reasons but to make money for the investors of the Virginia Company in the City of London, knows that America has very mixed origins. *Some* of the original colonies existed to enable religious freedom, but others most certainly did not. (Indeed there was no freedom of religion in Virginia until the 1780s, when the deist Thomas Jefferson persuaded the burgesses of that state to pass a statute enabling it.) Others, such as Massachusetts and Pennsylvania, allowed for people to practice their version of the Christian faith as they saw fit and in ways that the repressive regimes back home did not.

That is why Americans celebrate Thanksgiving, the annual ritual that goes back to the original first successful harvest of the Pilgrim fathers in Massachusetts, but not, by contrast, the first tobacco harvest sent back to Britain from Virginia by the colonists who went to the Commonwealth not to enjoy religious freedom but to make as much money as possible.

The Puritans in the New World, as many authors have shown, had what one might describe as an Old Testament view of themselves, of being like the children of Israel entering the Promised Land after centuries of oppression in Egypt. This was, I should add, a very *English* way of interpreting the Bible—Lutherans would also later immigrate to the infant North American colonies but without the same spiritual expectations—and this is something that British readers should always remember, since until comparatively recent times there were also plenty of folk in the United Kingdom, Christians very much included, who equally felt that England and its empire had a special place in the purposes of God. (We see similar themes in the eschatology of the Puritans; we examined in chapter 5 how their view of the millennium strongly influenced their self-belief in being the special agents of God's plans.)

To these settlers, they were God's people creating a new country out of the wilderness that would bring in a godly place that would have a unique role in the providence of God. Land and inhabitants were special, and had *spiritual purposes.*

This is now called *American exceptionalism*, the belief that the United States is somehow different from any other country and has a quite unique place in the world today—as a former US secretary of state put it, America is still the *necessary country.*

In the nineteenth century, when the young United States was still in the afterglow of the Second Great Awakening, this influenced the notion of *manifest destiny.* It was, if you like, an increasingly secular version of the Puritan idea that America was, to use the original phrase, a bright city shining upon a hill.

Nowadays, if as many as one third of Americans are evangelical, that means that two-thirds are not. But this view is still prevalent, and it was interesting to see how many Americans during the Bush presidency were often shocked when they discovered how deeply hated the United States had become in the world outside—or, as I, an honorary Virginian might put it, how misunderstood. America still thinks of itself idealistically as a country that always means the best, that is bringing goodness to a fallen world outside, coming like the cavalry to the rescue. So in recent years when many found out that that was not at all how outsiders perceived the United States any longer, the realization often came as a most unpleasant surprise.

(Since a McCain presidency might have restored America in the eyes of the outside world just as much as an Obama presidency, it is important to say that this is not a politically partisan point I am making. And as I pointed out earlier, many evangelical Americans, with numerous global contacts among evangelicals worldwide, were not at all surprised at how perceptions of their country had declined, especially, one might add, evangelical Republicans.)

All this, I argue, is closely linked to how *some* American evangelicals see themselves, and why others, such as Monsma, want to point out to their fellow evangelicals that an exceptionalist view of America is *theologically* wrong, let alone historically inaccurate.

For as Monsma correctly shows us, the view that the United States was once some glorious Christian country that needs to be reclaimed is, in fact, nonsense. Unfortunately, those who have bought into the *Christian America* myth are those upon whom the liberal media, in both Britain and the United States, concentrate, and are therefore the ones about whom we hear the most. What is encouraging, for those of us who are non-American evangelicals (the overwhelming majority of evangelicals, as this book makes clear) is that many American evangelicals are realizing this now too, and in ways that helpfully reconnect them to the evangelical majority outside of the United States, in places such as Nigeria or Brazil.

This is important, because the myth that America was once a glowing Christian country that wicked twentieth-century liberal humanists stole from us, and that now needs to be reclaimed by Christians re-imposing godly norms through political action, is just that—a myth.

For even by the seventeenth and early eighteenth centuries, the godly of Massachusetts had realized that while the founding fathers had been men and women of deep faith, that had already ceased to be the case with their current population. We see this in the book by Puritan scholar Cotton Mather, *The Great Works of Christ in America,* which was published as early as 1702. Mather decried the fact that the colonies were not as spiritually-minded as they had been just a few generations before, something that had also been conceded by the Massachusetts authorities in the Half-Way Covenant, which allowed nonchurch-going family members to be able to vote in state elections.[8]

Theologically, from an evangelical point of view, all this should not be at all surprising! If you recall the chapter on the distinctive nature of the evangelical interpretation of Scripture, you know that one of the

133

tenets of specifically *evangelical* belief is that each person is born again not because of family ties or geographical citizenship, but through an *individual* and personal faith in Jesus Christ as Savior and Lord. It is your own relationship with Jesus that saves you, not a godly parentage or being born into a historically Christian country. (And, indeed, most evangelicals in the world have ancestors who were pagan, living in countries in which Christianity was unknown until well into the nineteenth century.)

So one might say it is not *spiritually* surprising at all that even within a hundred years of the Pilgrim fathers, numerous of their descendants were no longer church-attending, professing Christians. You cannot inherit the faith of your parents; the Bible makes this clear time and again, in the Old Testament as well as in the New, for what was unfortunately true of the children of Israel was to be true of the church centuries later.

This, Steve Monsma demonstrates, is as theologically true as it is historically also the case. Yet part of the whole rationale of the religious right, as he shows in his book, is based precisely upon this false premise, that there once was a godly country that has been stolen, and that *through political action* American Christians can re-impose it, and therefore make God bless America once again.

But, one might add, one of the exciting things about the infant church, something that the book of Acts enthuses about again and again, is that *Christians are from all races under the sun.* This is what is new and exciting: *God's people are no longer geographically or ethnically restricted.* Even a despised Ethiopian eunuch can enter the kingdom of heaven as a full and equal member! Now, once again, in the twenty-first century, Christianity is returning to its Two-thirds World roots, with countless millions of people around the world becoming evangelical born-again believers in nations in which the Christian gospel has never before been proclaimed.

Therefore, for most evangelicals, the very idea of a *Christian country* is a theological impossibility: God's people are now everywhere! If one looks at the spiritual wilderness that is secular Europe, what is amazing in the United States is that there are still as many Christians as there are—as I was writing this chapter, I was also reading about how atheists now form the third biggest belief block in America, behind Baptists and Catholics.

How is it that Christianity grew in the first century? How has it grown by gigantic amounts in a country such as the People's Republic of China since 1951, when the Western missionaries were expelled? It certainly was not through legislation! Christianity grew exponentially despite all that Rome hurled against it in its early years, and the same is the case in Communist China today. In fact Christianity is often growing the most in countries where becoming a Christian can cost you your life, which was exactly the situation in New Testament times.

And now many leading American evangelicals are fully aware of this, no longer trusting in secular election victories to bring godliness to the United States. The newspaper you read may not realize this, and it may still spout all the old clichés, but the situation in the United States is changing, regardless of who sits in the White House.

So, I would argue, what the secular media think of as American *evangelicalism* does not actually reflect true *evangelical belief* at all. Rather it is American exceptionalism in religious garb, the belief that the United States is a special place given outwardly Christian clothes. The evangelical stereotype does not reflect true global evangelicalism, what the Bible teaches, or even what millions of American evangelicals believe themselves! With the old generation of the religious right dead or retired, *this* part of the mythology is now surely on the way out.

One could in fact say that during the days of the Moral Majority, many evangelicals forgot that it is *conversion*, as in the Great Awakening, that leads to moral change. They were trying, ironically considering that so many of their ancestors wished to flee religious persecution, to re-establish the pre-Reformation idea of *Christendom*, of compulsory Christianity, as once was interpreted by the Catholic Church, in which geography determined your belief, not *personal* conversion. Protestants initially went along with the idea of *Christendom*, Luther and Calvin included, but by the late seventeenth century Christians had realized that you cannot by definition coerce people into being *truly* Christian, because that fundamental change can only come from within, or, as evangelicals would say, as a result of the Holy Spirit working within someone's heart and mind.

One of the things that puzzled me back in the early eighties (when, as a publisher, I was reading many American books, including those on politics) was one of Tim LaHaye's many nonfiction works.[9] This particular volume had a chapter on how Christians ought to vote, and one of the key questions was: how did your senator/congressman vote on the Panama Canal issue? (This was written not long after President Carter signed the Panama Canal back to its original country.)

The Panama Canal?

I could see how, say, abortion, would be a key moral issue, and indeed it was one of those that LaHaye chose to discuss. But, I wondered, *how is a representative's vote on the Panama Canal something upon which evangelical Christians should decide how to vote*? What had the Panama Canal to do with the gospel, the sanctity of life, the importance of marriage and the family, and all those many issues upon which the Bible has clear teaching, and thus upon which Christians should be concerned with when they cast their ballots?

But the Panama Canal was, to this British outsider, an entirely political issue, one upon which Christians *as individuals* were entirely entitled to have strong views one way or another, but, unlike abortion or the sanctity of marriage, was not a spiritual issue upon which Christians should be told to vote one way or another. To me, this was an illegitimate use of Christian morality, imposing a partisan *secular* political viewpoint in the context of a *Christian* book.

All this, one can argue, was part and parcel of trying to establish a semitheocracy where it was not really possible. It also showed a misunderstanding of the link between Christianity and the state.

Christendom, therefore, from both a pragmatic viewpoint and from that of spiritual/biblical realities, cannot exist in a Protestant, let alone evangelical, framework. Geography, biological descent—neither are relevant to whether people become Christians. And, as British Puritans discovered in the seventeenth century and American evangelicals in the eighteenth, politics makes no difference here. God's people on earth are his church, and neither location nor genes count for admission.

So even from the point of view of sheer pragmatism, all attempts to enforce God's law on non-Christians, people who by spiritual definition *don't get it*, are bound to fail unless non-Christians too agree with the argument that Christians are putting forward. Even atheists agree that murder is wrong, so we have laws against that. But on many a moral issue, evangelicals are alas in a minority, and attempts to legislate for things that only Christians feel are wrong would lead not to righteousness but to another variant of Prohibition, where the law might say one thing but millions of Americans would behave as if such a law simply did not exist.

Win people over, however, as the abolitionists did in the nineteenth century, and things change dramatically.

Nonpartisan Attempts at Change

Evangelicals in the United States have recently rediscovered the Wilberforce way of doing things. I mentioned earlier that neither Wilberforce nor Shaftesbury—the latter not being so well known in the United States—organized their campaigns on *partisan* lines. Nor in fact did the nineteenth-century abolitionists in the United States. Campaigns now put together by evangelicals, such as those on the environment, human rights (including religious freedom but also the abolition of the *de facto* slavery that still exists in many parts of the world), AIDS, and other issues are doing what they can to get cross-party, broad-based support.

Britain saw this kind of support on the issue of trading on Sundays, where the Jubilee Centre, a major evangelical charity and campaigning organization, was successful, for a few years at least, in preventing legislation that would deregulate the hitherto very strict Sunday shop opening laws, with its campaign being called Keep Sunday Special. Many evangelicals wanted to keep Sunday for God, and wished to preserve legislation that did not oblige Christians to work on Sundays instead of going to church. Evangelicals also gained the strong support of the Trade Union Movement, who did not want its members to have to work unregulated hours on Sundays either. So there were Conservative and Labor Members of Parliament both working together to keep Sunday special—maybe for different reasons, but together and successfully all the same.

This is important: on some issues evangelicals are realizing that they need to campaign with people who do *not* agree with them politically.

137

Francis Schaeffer understood this in his concept of *cobelligerency*. He felt that though people might not agree with evangelicals spiritually, on particular issues they might be in full agreement with us, and they can help us campaign for specific issues, adding their voices to ours in public debate.

In Britain, for example, many church-going people, let alone evangelicals, are worried about what schools are teaching to young children in terms of moral views, and on that issue evangelical and, say, Catholic parents, find themselves in unity with Muslim parents, who are equally concerned.

Another example is the issue of debt forgiveness to developing countries. Evangelicals marched to support this campaign because of their interpretation of the Old Testament's Jubilee Principle, in which debts were forgiven in the forty-ninth year. Many of those marching with church groups in Britain were atheists or people of no fixed religious belief, whose reasons for joining in the campaign were thus very different from those of concerned evangelicals, for whom it was a moral and spiritual issue. But they could all march together all the same. (And I did not read of evangelicals saying that you were not an evangelical if you disagreed with debt forgiveness! This was how some evangelicals interpreted the Old Testament as *individual believers*, but they were not trying to make their view compulsory, as Tim LaHaye was doing with the Panama Canal, since they recognized that this was something about which many other evangelicals felt differently, as evangelicals often do on issues, such as baptism or church government. Scaremongering journalists in Britain who see a religious right coming to the United Kingdom are very far off the mark.)

In the recent past, many perceived the Moral Majority as putting forward specific platforms designed to benefit evangelicals only, or so Monsma and others now argue. While I imagine that many evangelicals in the United States would disagree with this analysis—and that is probably an understatement—nonetheless it was the powerful *outside* perception. But now, with the new generation of leaders wishing to join in campaigns to alleviate or even abolish poverty at home and abroad, to help conserve the environment, and to show human solidarity to those being persecuted by tyrannical regimes, the perception has strongly changed. Now even secular writers praise evangelicals for their powerful advocacy of the poor and oppressed in Africa, and for their active involvement too. So public perception of evangelicals is changing, as the nonreligious in the United States realize that evangelicals are involved in issues that all can support, and do so altruistically.

I should point out, as my younger informant was keen to mention, that to say the religious right has gone altogether is to write it off prematurely. He is probably right. And secular commentators are correct to say that there are certainly many thousands of evangelicals left *within* the Republican Party, as active as they always were, and for whom the hot-button issues such as abortion, gay marriage, and stem cell research are as vivid as ever. In fact, some analysts have even suggested that evangelicals within the Republican Party are now more powerful than before, in that as fewer Americans in general now support the Republicans (at least for the time being) the percentage of party activists who are evangelical is now higher than it was when that Party was more broadly constituted. This also means, of course, that post-2009, evangelicals will perhaps have a larger say in the internal debates within American conservatism on where to go next than might have been the case hitherto.

But one can say that the *nature* of the so-called religious right has changed, with overtly political pastors such as James Kennedy being replaced by younger men who focus more on proclaiming the truths of the gospel from their pulpits, rather than on politics. This new generation understands what the Bible itself teaches—the basis of all evangelical belief—that it is through *conversion*, through the inward change in the hearts and minds of individual people, that the church grows, and not on vain attempts to legislate God's kingdom by human means.

On moral issues, we also need to have practical backup, to make our position stronger. Many evangelicals have realized, for instance, that if you want to restrict abortion, it is vital to have effective postnatal care. As one American evangelical has commented, there is not much point in preventing abortions if there is no one to look after a child once it has been born and not aborted. Evangelicals should thus be as active in this area as secular liberals, and, for that matter, *even more so*, since liberals do not believe abortion is wrong.

However, that does not mean that evangelicals in the United States have retreated back into their safe hidey-holes—far from it! And it is to what they are doing and why that we shall now turn.

Some Specific Issues

It seems that one of the things that puzzled Michael Gerson, the Wheaton-educated evangelical speechwriter to George W. Bush, was that while there was quite a good deal of correspondence to the White House on the traditional hot button issues such as abortion, the major subject upon which evangelicals wrote in to their president was aid to and human rights in Africa, and Darfur in particular.[10] Significantly, even that president's sternest critics felt that whatever he got wrong, such as Iraq and the economy, he did get aid to Africa right, since he massively increased it during his time in office and took development assistance to that continent, and help to combat AIDS in particular, very seriously.

In addition, on the issue of birth control, as Monsma makes clear, evangelicals, being Protestants, do not have the same problem with preventing pregnancy that Catholics do (I wrote this when the pope was in enormous media trouble for trying to ban birth control devices in Africa). On abortion itself, Catholics and evangelicals are very much as one, but on this point they differ.

On a related issue, the evangelical position in the United States on stem cells, which does match that of the Catholic Church, is not always followed outside the United States. Many distinguished evangelicals in Britain, for instance, state that spare embryos, being artificial laboratory creations, are *not* people, with a soul and in the image of God, since the spare sperm, so to speak, in normal conception do not survive; the fact that they do only in a laboratory proves that the technical survivals of such sperm create embryos that are thus not living creatures. This is of course a mightily controversial issue on both sides of the Atlantic! But I remember going to a packed debate in Cambridge, England, where one of President Bush's advisers was arguing against stem cell research, and Sir Brian Heap, one of Britain's most eminent evangelical scientists and bioethicists, argued not on scientific but on *scriptural* grounds that a spare embryo was not, *biblically speaking,* a person with a soul who therefore had to be preserved.

Needless to say, most *American* evangelicals reading this will not agree with Sir Brian's views (and I am not giving my own), but once again we see that what is true in the United States is not always true elsewhere.

It was also interesting for your author, who has written on the Middle East and on the creation of Iraq, to read in the Monsma book that many evangelicals in the United States did not agree that the war in Iraq—as opposed to the war against Al Qaeda in Afghanistan—was correct, according to the *just war* theories that Christians have used to debate the rightness or wrongness of a war for centuries.

This shows that evangelicals are now not necessarily in lockstep with the Republican Party on whatever that party decides. This is also true with environmental issues, where evangelicals, who had been wary of the New Age mystical part of the Green Movement, have started to look at the issues themselves and, as Schaeffer hoped they would, look at them biblically. Evangelicals have always realized that Christians, and humans in general for that matter, should be good stewards, to use the scriptural term, of God's earth, going back to the mandate God gave in the book of Genesis. While not everyone agrees that global warming is a real phenomenon, and while even those who do believe it to be real disagree on what causes it, nevertheless evangelicals are waking up to the fact that the environment is not as it should be, and that they, as God's stewards for the planet, ought to act responsibly, whatever the truth might be. (In Britain there are many leading evangelicals on the scientific front, such as Sir John Houghton, former Director General of the UK Meteorological Office, in charge of government policy on climate change, and the son of one of the founders of the thoroughgoing Calvinist publisher the Banner of Truth! Sir John has written extensively on environmental concerns from both a secular and evangelical perspective, and in Britain, thankfully, these issues have not become party political football in the way they have in the United States.[11] The major parties disagree on *what* to do, but not on whether global warming exists, and this makes it much easier for evangelicals to decide on the issues themselves, since there is no ideological pull one way or the other.)

Once I had to write a book that included a chapter on energy policy, since one of the major issues in dealing with radical Islam is that so much of the world's petroleum is in parts of the Middle East, such as Saudi Arabia, that actively use their petro-dollars to fund extremist and anti-Western, anti-Christian Islam.[12] I wanted to call that chapter "Can Christians Drive an SUV?" That publisher said no, because so many Christians *did* drive SUVs, and they would be offended! So I was delighted to see in the Monsma book a discussion of that very subject—*should Christians drive gas-guzzling cars such as an SUV?* Monsma approached it from a different angle: was it environmentally responsible and in keeping with the biblical doctrine of good steward-ship for evangelicals to drive such vehicles? But he and I concluded the same thing! So whether evangelicals wish to drive responsibly or deny petro-dollars to kingdoms that oppose Christianity, the answer is identical: it is not wise for faithful evangelicals to be gas-guzzlers when they buy a car.

Evangelicals in the United States, as Monsma shows, are rethinking many issues like this *biblically*, which is what we ought to be doing, and in theory at least *should have* been doing since the Reformation, since we hold to the doctrine of *sola scriptura*, by Scripture alone (which we examined when we looked at the IFES basis of faith). Many will still conclude that Republican policy is right and continue to vote for that party based on such a generalization. But the link may no longer be *automatic*, or knee-jerk. Just because so many environmentalists are hippy-dippy New Agers or are pro-choice because they want to regulate population growth does not mean that evangelicals automatically reject global warming and support oil-drilling in Alaska. It is now perfectly possible to be pro-life and *biblically* pro-environment, as Francis Schaef-fer was arguing evangelicals should be back in the 1970s.[13]

This should also have the paradoxical effect of making evangelicals in the United States far more powerful than they were before! Politi-cians on *both* sides of the political divide will have to work for their votes, as has been the case in Britain and similar countries for a long time. While many evangelicals still feel that Obama was the "pro-death" candidate on the abortion issue, it is also true that for the first time since Carter, there was a Democratic candidate for whom evangelical votes actually mattered.

At the time of my writing this, there is no way, of course, of knowing how all this will pan out—and if the economy has disintegrated further by the time you read this, then it will not just be evangelicals who wonder if they can vote Democrat next time. But, in addition, the Republicans will have to woo evangelicals properly rather than simply seeing them as a bloc vote to be taken totally for granted. Evangelicals will no longer be able to be pawned off by clever phrases. They will want real action instead, and not just on the culture war issues but on the environment, overseas aid, and human rights.

America is no more evangelical or godly in 2009 than it was in 2001, and as we saw earlier, biblically speaking it is wrong for evangelicals to expect politicians to deliver what they need the Holy Spirit to grant. But at least evangelicals will be politically more realistic and know not to expect the moon from those who cannot deliver.

Afterword: The New Calvinism

In March 2009, Time magazine, America's major news weekly (along with *Newsweek*), listed ten trends that were changing, or going to change, the world in 2009.[1] Needless to say, some in other countries immediately protested that it was in *United States* where these hot trends were prevalent or actively being discussed. But since the United States is still the most powerful country in the world, with what happens there usually occurring in other places a few years later, what happens there is always of enormous interest to those living elsewhere.

Here are the ten trends of which we should all be aware. I list them here without comment, since one of them will surprise you, as it did the hundreds of thousands of people around the world who read *Time* each week:

What's Next 2009
1. Jobs Are the New Assets
2. Recycling the Suburbs
3. The New Calvinism
4. Reinstating the Interstate
5. Amortality
6. Africa, Business Destination
7. The Rent-A-Country
8. Biobanks

9. Survival Stores
10. Ecological Intelligence

Some of these were entirely new to me—what is *amortality* after all? Some are good news—such as the rediscovery of Africa as somewhere truly important after all, especially with the first ever president of African descent in the White House. *Ecological intelligence* is surely cutting-edge in our environmentally-aware world, and no more than a trendy way of saying that we have been more ecologically aware as we recycle our rubbish/garbage each week and consider taking the train instead of riding in a carbon-emitting car.

But look again at number 3: the New Calvinism.

Yes, we have read that correctly—new and twenty-first-century friendly forms of Reformed theology are what secular, mainstream *Time* magazine says is the number 3 new development to change life in America. Even Christian bloggers and commentators were amazed at this, particularly at the utter lack of condescension in the article (since many evangelicals have become almost paranoid at the attitudes of the secular press). And while news magazines do not always get their trend-spotting correctly, this time they were very much on target, since Reformed/evangelical Christianity is indeed very much on the rise in the United States today.

Two preliminary observations are needed.

First, one of the most significant things is that *Time* did not choose the trend most written about by academics, sociologists, and others: the so-called *emerging church* movement. Like postmodernism, to which it owes so much, the "emerging church" is hard to define, since, like postmodernism, it does not believe in absolutes. But as one of the movement's leading lights told *Christianity Today* writer Collin Hansen, we are all built on sand, and the very notion of firm foundations is by definition meaningless.

Suffice it to say here, the emergent movement can perhaps best be described as an effective surrender by post-evangelicals to the prevalent *zeitgeist* of our postmodern age. Rather than fighting the postmodernists, the emergent churches have given in, agreeing with their secular counterparts that in today's culture, the absolute is out and the relative is in.

For the theologically liberal end of the spectrum, this has come as good news, since the so-called mainline denominations made their surrender decades ago, though in their case to modernism and to the Enlightenment view that religion was now no longer tenable. It is not surprising, therefore, that their members among academia are interested in the emergent church, since the new trend is doing what the forefathers of today's liberals did at the end of the nineteenth and beginning of the twentieth centuries.

Second, we need to define *Calvinism*. Calvin had a wide breadth of beliefs, many of which appear in the creeds or confessions and catechisms written either in his lifetime or by his followers in the decades that followed. The Heidelberg Catechism, for example, is one of the best known today, and is still used in the twenty-first century by many churches of Presbyterian persuasion.

The most famous of all Calvin's distinctive doctrines was the doctrine of grace, which is the mechanism by which people become Christians. We will examine this shortly, but here we must note that Calvin believed in many other things as well, including, for example, infant baptism as part of what Presbyterians call covenant theology. To a Presbyterian— in, say, the Church of Scotland in Britain or the PCA in the United States, baptism is the New Testament equivalent of circumcision in the Old, something that happens to you shortly after birth, though in the case of baptism, to girls as well as to boys. According to covenant theology, to be baptized you must have Christian parents who are full, believing, and practicing members of the church where you have your baptism. The evangelical wing of Presbyterianism would not approve of the belief in many Anglican/Episcopal churches that says that whoever is born in the parish has the right to be baptized.

During the Reformation, this went from being a mainstream view to one held principally by those on the Reformed, or Calvin-following, side of Protestantism. What we now call Baptists emerged in the seventeenth century.

But, as Collin Hansen's book, *Young, Restless, Reformed: A Journalist's Journey with the New Calvinists* shows us, today many Baptists are also calling themselves *Reformed*, and, in fact, most of the leadership of the group that *Time* magazine calls the New Calvinism are Baptists, notably Mark Dever, whose 9Marks we examined elsewhere, along with John Piper in Minnesota, Al Mohler in Kentucky, and John MacArthur in California.[2]

So there are *Calvinist Baptists*—or are there?

For some strongly evangelical Calvinists—such as well-known radio personality and seminary professor Mike Horton—the mix is impossible. By definition, a Baptist disagrees strongly with Calvin over who should be baptized and why, since in Baptist theology, baptism takes place *after* conversion to Christian faith, and thus, almost inevitably, when the baptismal candidate is older, quite often an adult.

However, all the Baptists that I have just mentioned would strongly disagree (as would your author), since what distinguishes *Reformed theology* from that of other branches of evangelicalism, or indeed other parts of the Protestant spectrum, is the belief that the Bible teaches *the doctrines of grace.* To this new, or neo-Calvinist way of thinking, *this* is the key tenet, and the fact that people within the Reformed world differ from each other (and as we see, often from Calvin himself) on the issue of baptism is of secondary importance.

According to this thinking, it is thus possible to be a Calvinist, or a believer in Reformed theology, without having to subscribe to the whole Reformation package of both Calvin himself and, in an American context, the equally important legacy that he bequeathed to his English-speaking followers in Britain and the New World: the Puritans.

This takes us back to chapter 4, where we looked at the history of evangelicalism, particularly the Reformation rediscovery of the doctrine of *sola scriptura* or Scripture alone. Why do we believe what we do? *We do so because that is what the Bible teaches.* "Scripture alone" is at the very heart of the Protestant's, and in the twenty-first century, the evangelical's, belief, and is one of the key distinctions between Catholicism and Protestantism. There is no Protestant equivalent of the pope, and there are, as is obvious from looking down many a street, a plethora of Protestant denominations that differ with each other on what Luther called secondary or indifferent issues but who share the same core beliefs of who Jesus is and what he came to do. As we also examined, specifically *evangelical* bases of faith have the core doctrines and tenets in which *all* evangelicals believe, even if they differ wildly from one another on issues such as baptism, church government, the way in which to worship, and more besides.

So what the New Calvinists are saying (and I would agree with them) is that *if you define Reformed or Calvinist theology by the doctrines of grace, then even Baptists can be Calvinists.* How is this possible if Calvin differed? The answer is that Calvin himself believed, along with all the great sixteenth- and seventeenth-century Reformers, *that the Bible determines belief.* This means that evangelical Presbyterians and evangelical Baptists can believe equally that Calvin was right about the doctrines of grace, even if they then go on to differ on whether he was right in his view of baptism.

As I mentioned earlier, not all evangelicals in Presbyterian denominations would agree. But many do, including those included in what both *Time* and Hansen's *Young, Restless, Reformed* would call the New Calvinists.

So let us look first at what this is all about doctrinally, then at how there are not just Baptists but also charismatic evangelicals among the New Calvinists (in Britain as well as in the United States), and finally at how Calvinism is becoming one of the hottest beliefs among students and twenty-somethings all over the United States, with Calvinist African-American rappers taking the music world by storm!

The New Calvinists' Theology

Here I have to be careful, since as this is a book about evangelicals and I am one of their number, I do not want to appear factional within the movement. So this is a more cautious definition of Reformed theology than I would normally give.

But in essence, Reformed theology emphasizes the transcendent nature of God, his glory and his sovereign power, and his grace toward us as sinners. (This is why one of the biggest networks of Reformed churches in the United States is called *Sovereign Grace*). It stresses God's mercy and the wonder that any of us are saved at all, considering that all of us are by nature rebels against a Holy God.

Naturally, Reformed evangelicals believe what they do because that is what they see in Scripture. Needless to say, other evangelicals who interpret the Bible differently do not agree; they are often called Arminians, after the Dutch Reformation theologian Arminius, and today those of Methodist or Holiness persuasion would be firmly in the Arminian camp. And it is important as always to say that evangelicals of both viewpoints happily come together in evangelical solidarity on issues such as *soteriology*, the doctrine of the all-sufficient saving power of Jesus Christ upon the cross. It is also necessary to say that evangelicals in some denominations disagree among themselves on this issue of Reformed theology, notably in the Southern Baptist Convention, with some members of the recent evangelical resurgence, as it is called, aligned with John Wesley and Arminius and others with George Whitefield and John Calvin.

Nonetheless I think it's fair to say that Reformed evangelicals have a different emphasis, which, as the distinguished Anglican Calvinist evangelical theologian J. I. Packer argued in his book *Evangelism and the Sovereignty of God,* gives them a much stronger basis for evangelism than the Arminian position.[3] For the latter, human response is everything; for the former, the work of the Holy Spirit in convicting people of the need to repent and convert to Christian faith enables ordinary Christians sharing the gospel to know that with God helping them, no barrier can ever be powerful enough to prevent someone from both hearing the good news of Jesus Christ and responding to it positively.[4]

Reformed theology is often summarized by the acronym TULIP. Some of what follows are complex theological terms, so I will aim here to translate them into simpler English (as African-American rap lyricists now do, making Reformed theology cool in their communities for the first time).

T stands for *total depravity*. It means that we are *all* sinners, and that no deed we do can ever be good enough to get us into heaven. This, when preached in the twenty-first century, is entirely counter-cultural, since we are always being told today that we need to feel good about ourselves, to enjoy high self-esteem, and that God exists to meet our felt needs. **T** shows this is all rubbish. Hansen's fascinating book makes clear that it is precisely the fact that modern young people (who are flocking to Reformed youth meetings in the thousands) know this to be true of themselves—that they are *not* good enough—which gives Reformed theology the growing credibility it enjoys with so many intelligent twenty-somethings today.

U stands for *unconditional election*. It means that there is thus no merit in ourselves when God showers his love and grace upon us; our salvation is all because of God's grace rather than anything special on our part.

L stands for *limited atonement*. It is a simple demonstration that not everyone responds to the gospel. But despite the fact that we are by nature against God, he in his infinite mercy and grace nonetheless reaches out to save some of us, when in fact none of us deserve his forgiveness at all. (To say that there is a straight Arminian/Calvinist divide can be confusing here, since many evangelicals refer to themselves as "four-point" Calvinists or followers of "TUIP," believing in "T," "U," "I," and "P," but having problems with "L." But I think that this is not the place to elaborate on that point!)

I stands for *irresistible grace*. It focuses on the work of the Holy Spirit in the lives of those hearing the gospel, actively convicting people of their sinfulness and the need for salvation, rather than God being entirely passive, sitting in heaven, as it were, and hoping people will sign up.

P stands for *perseverance of the saints*. In essence it means that once God has got hold of you, he does not let you go! Becoming and living as a Christian is not solely about a one-time decision we make, but it is a process in which God plays the major role, for we are people who would never see the need to become a Christian if left to our own devices.

It is this feeling of certainty in troubled, postmodern times that Collin Hansen in *Young, Restless, Reformed* reports as making Reformed theology so innately appealing to younger evangelicals today: a safe mooring on a troubled sea, to use an analogy of my own.

One of the problems of much of Protestant Christianity today is that, as J. I. Packer would aver, it *reflects the culture rather than running counter to it*. Non-Christians want the warm-fuzzies, and so many megachurches today respond to that by telling the congregations how great they are! But this is completely contrary to what the Bible teaches, however virtuous we might think ourselves, as the Pharisees did in the time of Jesus. Actually we are rebels against God, *by nature* unworthy of his love and forgiveness. As a modern Christian lyric begins, "Only by Christ can we enter."

So as Hansen shows, thousands of young Americans go from Sunday schools at home that are doctrine-lite, having no in-depth teaching of any kind, to secular universities dominated by postmodernism and an entirely non-Christian worldview, and they suddenly find that they have no defenses! They have never actually *thought* through what they believe and why. Then they meet evangelical students who really have wrestled with the deep issues of life and have a profoundly rooted way of looking at life, their studies, relationships, and much else besides, and they find themselves thinking, *"Eureka! Christianity makes sense after all!"*

This is why conferences such as Passion are drawing students and young adults in the thousands. It is not the charisma of the preaching, since Reformed evangelicalism in the United States tends not to draw (thankfully?) the kind of slick salesman personalities so famous on television and in airport bookstores. It is the quality of the message and the lifestyle that goes with it that draw such large audiences, as well as the sheer intellectual integrity of the message combined with the zeal with which it is proclaimed.

This echoes the views of Dr. D. Martyn Lloyd-Jones, who was part of a similar renaissance of interest in Reformed theology in Britain after the Second World War. He referred to preaching as *logic on fire* or as *theology coming through a man who is on fire.* He was nicknamed the "last of the great Calvinistic Methodists," since he had the logic of Calvin and the fire of Methodism. Much modern preaching is either fiery with no thought behind it or coldly logical without emotion, but from the Puritans onward much of the Reformed tradition has encompassed both, with an appeal equally to heart and head, mind as well as emotion.

Charismatic New Calvinists

What is especially interesting in this regard is that the Reformed renaissance has a charismatic/Pentecostal wing, something wholly new in the history of Calvinism. This phenomenon is transatlantic, with a small movement in Britain called New Frontiers and a similar group in the United States, Sovereign Grace, led by the East Coast preacher C. J. Mahaney, a convert to Protestantism and its evangelical branch from a Roman Catholic background. Here Reformed theology and young people reading seventeenth-century Puritan tomes combine with the exuberant worship and loud music we associate with charismatic churches in mainstream groups and Pentecostal denominations across the world. Rocking to Calvinism may seem strange to some, but the growing number of churches in the Sovereign Grace network shows that it is indeed more than possible.

For some of Mahaney's former Pentecostal cohorts, his becoming Reformed in theology is going a step too far. Likewise, for many in quieter, more traditional Presbyterian and similar churches, having a charismatic in their midst, proclaiming that he is one of them in his enthusiasm for Reformed theology, is also a major culture shock. There are those, as we have seen, who have problems with people declaring themselves to be both Calvinist and Baptist, and now for there to be a large movement that says it is both Calvinist *and charismatic* is something that they find hard to accept.

Nonetheless, even those who are firmly of the view that the miraculous sign gifts, such as prophecy and speaking in tongues (in what one can describe as a heavenly, nonhuman language), passed away in Bible times are now welcoming Mahaney and others to their conferences and network meetings. One of the most eminent of these is John MacArthur. Because of his radio ministry he is one of the best-known preachers in the United States, but he is also controversial, since his book *Charismatic Chaos* shows that he is very much in what is called the *cessationist* camp, believing that the sign gifts have long since ceased.[5] MacArthur has one of the biggest conferences for pastors in North America, and Mahaney has spoken there (along with Mark Dever).

This is a symbol of how those who differ, often quite strongly, on some doctrinal issues nevertheless do come together on the important things that unite them. Mark Dever has also developed Together for the Gospel, a network of leaders who are both evangelical and Reformed. At Together for the Gospel conferences, one can see Baptists, an independent, a Presbyterian, and a charismatic all on the stage together.

New Calvinism among Students and Young People

In the United States, the student evangelism branch of the PCA, Reformed University Fellowship (RUF), now has a large and growing presence on many US campuses, including those of secular universities and colleges. By no means are all the students that attend RUF from PCA homes; many of them are from churches and denominations that would firmly reject Reformed theology. (Hansen tells a story of teenagers who got in trouble with their youth pastor for reading Jonathan Edwards. So they switched instead to John Owen, an eminent seventeenth-century Puritan from Britain, because their church would not know who he was! If teenage rebellion now comes to reading the sermons of people who died nearly four hundred years ago, then times have *truly* changed.)

In Britain, students from New Frontiers churches normally join the main evangelical campus body, the UCCF (Universities and Colleges Christian Fellowship), and not the overtly charismatic group, Fusion, which has its origins in an evangelistically and socially dynamic south-coast group called Revelation Christian Fellowship, a network of churches in which many bikers, hippies, Goths, and similar kinds of "outcasts" found faith. While many New Frontiers students agree with Fusion on charismatic gifts, they identify strongly with the Reformed theological emphasis of their fellow UCCF members, even though many of the latter are cessationist on the issue of the miraculous gifts.

Once again, common attachment to Reformed theology trumps denominational ties for the upcoming future leaders of evangelicalism on both sides of the Atlantic.

Some of the Reformed renaissance is controversial even within the movement. The person to whom this most applies is Mark Driscoll, of Mars Hill Church in Seattle. (Mars Hill was the Roman version of the Araeopagus in Athens from which the apostle Paul preached a famous sermon that is featured in the book of Acts.)

Driscoll was originally part of the emerging church movement, but soon despaired of the mush that prevailed. He then discovered Reformed theology, and has never looked back. A small church of just a few hundred became one of thousands, and Driscoll is now one of the best-known members of the new Calvinist movement—indeed his blog is called the Resurgence.

Like the Revelation Christian Fellowship network in Britain (which is zealously Arminian), Driscoll has mainly reached out to the denizens of alternative America, for whom Seattle has acted as a powerful magnet. It is not often that you spot folk with tattoos in church, eagerly devouring a sermon—and one lasting over an hour at that—but at Mars Hill, this is quite common. People who would never have been seen in a more conventional church pour into Mars Hill every Sunday, as Collin Hansen describes in his book.

However, it is Driscoll's language that is most controversial. He does not hesitate to use the rough parlance of the streets, with fart jokes and analogies that are shocking even to those who are open to the need to speak to potential converts in a language to which they can relate. Hard-line Presbyterian churches are alas often described as the "frozen chosen," with their devotion to the Puritans leading them to speaking, preaching, and maybe even thinking in ways that we would call Shakespearean. What most of the Reformed renaissance would do is to find ways of outreach to the culture that are both decent and accessible to those unfamiliar with biblical terminology, which nowadays would be most of the population, whether mainstream or alternative.

But the issue of the salty language at Mars Hill hides that, along with many churches in the Reformed renaissance, it is profoundly and actively evangelistic. In the days of evangelistic giants such as Jonathan Edwards in North America and George Whitefield both there and in Britain, no one would have doubted for a minute that Calvinist theology and evangelism would be anything other than an obvious combination. (Indeed most objective biographies of Calvin show that no one was more zealous in spreading the gospel than Calvin himself, who sent thousands of brave missionaries from Geneva to France, despite Protestantism being persecuted by the French kings.)

However, in more recent years, this was not always perceived to be the case. This criticism was mainly a caricature, but there had always been enough "frozen chosen" to give some small substance to the claim. Now that is clearly no longer the case, with evangelism being a strong priority across all the churches of the renaissance, Baptist, charismatic, independent, and Presbyterian alike.

In addition, while *Time* uses the moniker "Neo-Calvinists," the people themselves prefer to think of their movement as being Scripture-based, rather than centered on the teachings of a particular historical individual, however critical his theology and influence might have been. Both Jonathan Edwards and George Whitefield did not use the description "Calvinist" of themselves, and nor do many of those in the Reformed renaissance today.

As Collin Hansen puts it in his seminal 2006 article in *Christianity Today*:

> Evangelicals have long disagreed on election and free will. The debate may never be settled, given the apparent tension between biblical statements and the limits of our interpretive skills. In addition, some will always see more benefit in doctrinal depth than others.
>
> Those fearing a new pitched battle can rest easy. That's not because the debate will go away—for the foreseeable future, the spread of Calvinism will force many evangelicals to pick sides. And it's not because mission will trump doctrine—young people seem to reject this dichotomy.
>
> It's because the young Calvinists value theological systems far less than God and his Word. Whatever the cultural factors, many Calvinist converts respond to hallmark passages like Romans 9 and Ephesians 1. "I really don't like to raise any banner of Calvinism or Reformed theology," said Eric Lonergan, a 23-year-old University of Minnesota graduate. "Those are just terms. I just like to look at the Word and let it speak for itself."
>
> That's the essence of what Joshua Harris [now senior pastor of C. J. Mahaney's church in Maryland] calls "humble orthodoxy." He reluctantly debates doctrine, but he passionately studies Scripture and seeks to apply all its truth.
>
> "If you really understand Reformed theology, we should all just sit around shaking our heads going, 'It's unbelievable. Why would God choose any of us?'" Harris said. "You are so amazed by grace, you're not picking a fight with anyone, you're just crying tears of amazement that should lead to a heart for lost people, that God does indeed save, when he doesn't have to save anybody."[6]

As to what will become of this movement, it is impossible at this stage to say. Certainly a group that can get forty thousand university students to spend a week at a conference studying theology in depth, getting deep into Bible study, and reading seventeenth- and eighteenth-century tomes is a remarkable phenomenon! Likewise, a movement that brings together Baptists, charismatics, and Presbyterians, as well as white Anglo-Saxons and black African-Americans (in a country where Sunday is often the most segregated day of the week) is truly impressive.

Even strongly Arminian evangelicals, such as those interviewed by Hansen at seminaries that reject Reformed theology in all its forms, are deeply struck by the zeal, commitment to evangelism, and biblical enthusiasm of the "young, restless, and Reformed." For in a day of postmodern mush, with relativism dominating campuses and belief itself being passé, these converts to Reformed evangelicalism really do believe something, even if their Arminian fellow evangelicals feel uncomfortable with some of their doctrinal distinctives.

Back in the 1940s a similar renaissance among students took place in Wales—on a much smaller scale, but powerful nonetheless. The movement it spawned is still going sixty-plus years later, but while it has certainly had an impact, it is not a strong British-wide phenomenon. The danger of a new generation of Reformed Americans lapsing into the "frozen chosen" mentality of earlier generations in Wales and the United States is always possible. The exciting awakening can become lost in factionalism and a kind of spiritual snobbery of the kind to which *Time* magazine alluded, if things turn out wrongly.

But while that is sadly bound to be a danger, human nature being what it is, for now the fact that the next generation of evangelicals is discovering the joys of Bible study, of standing up for evangelical truth on the secular campuses of the United States, of engaging in life-changing evangelism in places such as Chicago and New Orleans, of interracial churches and gatherings, and of actually trying to engage with and change the dominant culture without surrendering to it, is truly exciting and shows that evangelicalism is going to be around and dynamic even in the West, and for a long while yet.

Appendix

Pew Survey on Religion in the United States

In 2009 the Pew Forum on Religion & Public Life released a report that suggested that the number of nonreligious in the United States had grown in recent years.[1] In many publications the headline news was that 16 percent of Americans no longer had any kind of religious faith. Other commentators picked up on the statistics of how many Roman Catholics had left their church of origin and the number of Protestants who now had a different kind of expression from their original Protestant affiliation. One leading Southern Baptist noticed that New England, the original Puritan heartland, was now far from religion of any kind.

Needless to say, some in the secular press took this news with much rejoicing, writing off religion in the United States as increasingly a thing of the past, because nonbelievers in the United States had more than doubled in recent years, from 7 percent to 16. However, it is worth taking a proper look at the real implications of the report, especially from an *evangelical* point of view.

First of all, for *only* 16 percent of Americans, the most technologically advanced democracy in the Western world, to have no faith of *any* kind looks drastically different if we look at it from a Western European angle. On the other side of the pond, atheism, agnosticism, and absence from church—even at Christmas or Easter—is rapidly becoming the norm as secularization marches effortlessly onward. But as we examined earlier, the United States is not really part of the West when it comes to religion, and is far more similar to those countries in the Two-thirds World where religious belief of *some* kind or another remains the norm. If 16 percent of Americans have no religious inclination, then *84 percent still do*, which for a modernized industrial country in the twenty-first century is still extraordinary.

What we are seeing too in the statistics about Catholics leaving their churches is not the end of religion as the Puritans would have understood it, but the end of nominal faith—many Catholics call it "cradle Catholicism," where one is a Catholic by culture and ancestry but certainly not by practice, except perhaps for weddings or funerals.

Not only would the same apply to the old mainline Protestant denominations—though the term "cradle Protestant" has never existed as such—but, as we saw elsewhere, *this has been the case since the early eighteenth century.* It is the rationale, as I have shown, for *The Great Works of Christ in America* by Cotton Mather, who already saw that the descendants of the early Protestant founding fathers were no longer truly active in their supposed faith.

In other words, what we are seeing is nothing new.

What we are seeing is the end of nominal/cultural Christianity, and from an evangelical point of view that is not a bad thing, since one of the factors that inoculates people best against evangelical Christianity is thinking that they are Christians already, by virtue of where they live. (Incidentally, the notion that the northeastern United States is no longer its original Puritan self is far from being news, as Cotton Mather realized over three hundred years ago. When I was the guest of the Billy Graham organization for a Crusade back in the early 1980s, it was fascinating to hear the team say that they far preferred being in the Northeast, where Americans knew they were not Christians, than in the South, where people felt you could be a born-again Baptist from physical birth!)

One of the main goals of the Protestant Reformation back in the sixteenth century was to break up the medieval idea of Christendom: that being born in, say, England or Denmark made you a Christian. The whole notion was emphatically rejected by the Reformers, who made it abundantly clear from Scripture that to become a Christian *you had to be born again personally*, and that the geographical location in which your physical birth took place made not the slightest difference to your relationship with God and to your salvation. That is why, elsewhere in this book, I try to get away from the notion of "Christian America," however appealing that idea might be for cultural or political reasons.

So in reality what is happening is that people who did not really believe anything anyway, whatever their culturally Christian background, are no longer making any pretense. From the point of view of whether or not they have the kind of saving faith upon which evangelicals insist, the *real* difference is negligible.

The statistic on those changing Protestant denominations is also, from an evangelical standpoint, essentially meaningless. If someone goes from a theologically liberal so-called mainline denomination and begins attending a lively evangelical church of different denominational persuasion, that is actually good news rather than bad. They have become fed up with mush and want the real thing!

As for changes of denomination *within an evangelical framework,* in effect no change has happened at all. If, for example, a family moves to a new house and goes from an *evangelical* Southern Baptist church in Town X but finds that in Town Y the best evangelical church is, say, PCA, then while the Pew survey has them changing denominations (which they are), from the family's point of view no significant change has happened, because they have simply gone from one evangelical church to another. For, as we saw, while evangelicals do not dismiss denominational differences—Baptists are Baptists, and Presbyterians are still Presbyterians—*ultimately* evangelical loyalty and unity trump denominational distinctions every time. And now, for example, many evangelical parishes within the Church of England are baptizing adults by believer's immersion, proving that denominational differences are becoming increasingly irrelevant in any case.

Finally, as even the very secular and politically/theologically liberal British newspaper *The Guardian* commented, what the Pew survey does not show is that people in the United States are ceasing to be *religious* but are now expressing their faith differently. Instead of believing in nineteenth-century modernist theological liberalism, what the old mainline denominations believe in, ordinary Americans are turning to belief in numerous impossible things before breakfast! Look at a bookstore in the United States and one will find that the shelves of New Age and similar books are groaning with countless books, many of which are bestsellers, all full of touchy-feely nonsense to make people feel good, especially in economically bad times.

So from an evangelical angle, such folk are just moving from one kind of waffle to another, except that, of course, they might now be easier to evangelize, since they no longer make any claim to be *Christian*.

Thus, the 2009 survey is not the bad news that many commentators have claimed.

Notes

Chapter 1: Some Core Evangelical Beliefs

1. See http://www.ifesworld.org.

2. Christopher Catherwood, *Church History: A Crash Course for the Curious*, rev. ed. (Wheaton, IL: Crossway, 2007).

3. Martyn Lloyd-Jones, *The Cross: God's Way of Salvation*, ed. Christopher Catherwood (Westchester, IL; Crossway, 1986).

4. 1 Peter 2:4–5, 9.

5. See statistical information at http://www.cia.gov and http://www.uscirf.gov/.

Chapter 2: A Typical Evangelical Church's Vision Statement

1. For more information on Alpha Course, see http://uk.alpha.org/ and http://www.alphana.org/.

2. Mark Dever, *Nine Marks of a Healthy Church*, rev. ed. (Wheaton, IL: Crossway, 2004).

3. Charles W. Colson, *Born Again* (Old Tappan, NJ: Fleming Revell, 1976; Grand Rapids: Chosen, 2008).

4. See especially Michael Horton, *Christless Christianity: The Alternative Gospel of the American Church* (Grand Rapids: Baker, 2008).

Chapter 3: Who Are Evangelicals?

1. http://www.ifesworld.org/.

2. Philip Jenkins, *The Next Christendom: The Coming of Global Christianity*, rev. ed. (Oxford; New York: Oxford University Press, 2007); *The New Faces of Christianity: Believing the Bible in the Global South* (Oxford; New York: Oxford University Press,

2006); *God's Continent: Christianity, Islam, and Europe's Religious Crisis* (Oxford; New York: Oxford University Press, 2007); *The Lost History of Christianity: The Thousand-Year Golden Age of the Church in the Middle East, Africa, and Asia—and How It Died* (New York, HarperOne, 2008). (I am unable to give precise references to every thought or statistic that I received from my profitable readings of Professor Jenkins's quartet.)

3. Mark Juergensmeyer, *Terror in the Mind of God: The Global Rise of Religious Violence* (Berkeley: University of California Press, 2000).

4. Michael Brooks, "Natural Born Believers: How Your Brain Creates God," *New Scientist* 201: 2694 (February 7, 2009): 32.

5. David B. Barrett, George T. Kurian, and Todd M. Johnson, *World Christian Encyclopedia: a comparative survey of churches and religions in the modern world,* 2nd ed. (Oxford; New York: Oxford University Press, 2001); *World Christian Handbook* (London: World Dominion Press, 1949–1968).

Chapter 4: Evangelicals Past and Present

1. Mark A. Noll, David W. Bebbington, George A. Rawls, eds. *Evangelicalism: Comparative Studies of Popular Protestantism in North America, the British Isles, and Beyond, 1700–1990* (New York: Oxford University Press, 1994).

2. John Stott, *Evangelical Truth: A Personal Plea for Unity, Integrity & Faithfulness,* 2nd ed. (Downers Grove, IL: InterVarsity, 2003), 15.

3. Christopher Catherwood, *Church History: A Crash Course for the Curious,* rev. ed. (Wheaton, IL: Crossway, 2007).

4. *Amazing Grace,* dir. Michael Apted, FourBoys Films, 2007.

5. D. W. Bebbington, *Evangelicalism in Modern Britain: A History from the 1730s to the 1980s* (London; Boston: Unwin Hyman, 1989), 120.

6. Nancy Gibbs and Michael Duffy, "Billy Graham: 'A Spiritual Gift to All,'" *Time,* May 31, 2007.

7. Christopher Catherwood, *Five Evangelical Leaders* (Wheaton, IL: Harold Shaw, 1985).

8. See John Stott, *The Lausanne Covenant: An Exposition and Commentary* (Wheaton, IL: Lausanne Committee for World Evangelism, 1975).

Chapter 5: Trials and Tribulations

1. Tim LaHaye and Jerry Jenkins, Left Behind series (Wheaton, IL: Tyndale, 1995–2007).

2. Iain H. Murray, *The Puritan Hope: A Study in Revival and the Interpretation of Prophecy* (London: Banner of Truth, 1971).

3. See, for example, Nicholas D. Kristof, "Following God Abroad," *New York Times,* May 21, 2002.

Chapter 6: The Minefield: A Survey of Evangelical Politics

1. Jim Wallis, God's Politics: *Why the Right Gets It Wrong and the Left Doesn't Get It* (San Francisco: HarperSanFrancisco, 2005).

2. Steve Monsma, *Healing for a Broken World: Christian Perspectives on Public Policy* (Wheaton, IL: Crossway, 2007).

3. John MacArthur, *Why Government Can't Save You* (Nashville: Word, 2000).

4. Rick Warren, *The Purpose-Driven Life: What on Earth Am I Here For?* (Grand Rapids: Zondervan, 2002).

5. Charles W. Colson, *Born Again* (Old Tappan: NJ: Fleming Revell, 1976; Grand Rapids: Chosen, 2008).

6. Ronald J. Sider, *Rich Christians in an Age of Hunger: A Biblical Study* (Downers Grove, IL: Intervarsity, 1977).

7. Walter McDougall, *Promised Land, Crusader State: The American Encounter with the World Since 1776* (Boston: Houghton Mifflin, 1997).

8. Cotton Mather, *The Great Works of Christ in America*, 3rd ed. (Edinburgh; Carlisle, PA: Banner of Truth, 1979).

9. Tim LaHaye, *The Battle for the Mind* (Grand Rapids: Baker, 1980) 77.

10. Michael Gerson, *Heroic Conservatism: Why Republicans Need to Embrace America's Ideals (and Why They Deserve to Fail If They Don't)* (New York: HarperOne, 2007).

11. See for example his *Global Warming: The Complete Brief,* 4th ed. (Cambridge; New York: Cambridge University Press, 2009).

12. See my *Christians, Muslims, and Islamic Rage: What Is Going On and Why It Happened* (Grand Rapids: 2003).

13. See Schaeffer and C. Everett Coop, *Whatever Happened to the Human Race?* (Old Tappan, NJ: Revell, 1979); Schaeffer, *Pollution and the Death of Man* (Wheaton, IL: Tyndale, 1970).

Afterword: The New Calvinism

1. *Time*, March 23, 2009, 45–66.

2. Collin Hansen, *Young, Restless, Reformed: A Journalist's Journey with the New Calvinists* (Wheaton, IL: Crossway, 2008).

3. J. I. Packer, *Evangelism and the Sovereignty of God* (Downers Grove, IL: InterVarsity Press, 1961, 2008).

4. *Evangelism and the Sovereignty of God* remains in print over half a century after it first appeared and is still an ideal guide to Reformed theology in plain English.

Packer is one of the grandfather figures of the Reformed renaissance in the United States and of evangelicals within the Anglican Communion worldwide.

5. John MacArthur, *Charismatic Chaos* (Grand Rapids: Zondervan, 1992).

6. Collin Hansen, "Young, Restless, Reformed," *Christianity Today*, September 22, 2006.

Appendix: Pew Survey on Religion in the United States

1. See http://pewforum.org/surveys/.